EMBRACING LIFE'S UNPREDICTABLE JOURNEY

NAVIGATING UPS AND DOWNS

ANURAG VIJAY

Made with ❤ on the Notion Press Platform
www.notionpress.com

Contents

Acknowledgements v

Introduction vii

Part 1
People And Need Of People 3

Part 2
Anger 17

Part 3
Friends And Friendship 31

Part 4
Greed 43

Part 5
Attachment 59

Part 6
Jealousy 73

Part 7
Pride 89

Part 8
Negativity 107

Part 9
Happiness 121

Part 10
Love 135

Part 11
Karma 147

SOURCES 155

Acknowledgements

This book is dedicated to my revered Guru Shree Kripalu Ji Maharaj. Introduced to his teachings in 2015 by a friend shortly after my father's passing, I regret not having met him in person, as he had already transcended to the heavenly realm. His profound wisdom has etched an enduring mark on my soul, profoundly shaping my perspective and enriching my life. These teachings offer an extraordinary path to navigate human existence. They've not only inspired me but encouraged me to share these invaluable insights with a wider audience. Sharing our passions fosters connections and nurtures communities built on shared values. Continuously absorbing his discourses, I strive to integrate his teachings into my daily life. My gratitude extends to my friend who introduced me to his teachings. Embracing even a fraction of his ideologies, I believe, has the power to transform our lives.

I extend heartfelt thanks to my wife Neha and the positive influences in my life, whose support and inspiration have fuelled the creation of this book.

INTRODUCTION

Life is a journey, not a destination. A very short one full of unpredictability. A multifarious emotional journey filled with love, happiness, sadness, attachment, resentment, jealousy, and a lot of varied emotions. As we navigate through this journey called life sometimes, we are prepared, and other times we are not. Life is full of unpredictable twists and turns, and it can be difficult to know when we'll be prepared for what comes our way. Sometimes we have all the tools we need to navigate a challenge, while other times we feel completely unprepared. Nonetheless, it is important to remember that every experience - good or bad - can be an opportunity to learn and grow.

We are fascinated to see how life can be complicated and, in some moments, even very easy. When everything's going our way, we start to be egotistic. If everything's wrong with us, we blame everyone else and curse our luck.

Humans are thinking creatures. We've got a gift to think, but what will happen if we overdo it? Our lives are made easier or harder by our environment, but it's us who make them that way. As children, adults, and professionals, we all have a lot of hurdles to overcome in our lives. It's making us unhappy and changing our perception of life.

We're frequently thinking we've made a lot of mistakes. We've challenged our belief in life. Life throws us off-balance by giving us a challenge when we feel too arrogant about something, when we feel too dejected life cheers us up and lifts our spirit by tossing something good our way. If we continue to have good things happening to us, we will die of a heart attack. Similarly, if we continue to have only bad stuff happening to us, we will die of a heart attack. We're going to be blown up in both cases.

We have the tendency to look at the good side of others and feel bad about the bad things happening to us. Life is not the same for everyone. God keeps us at a healthy balance by providing opportunities and challenges, good times, and adverse ones. And that's the way we go about our lives. If we learn to remain indifferent in both situations, we will not feel sad when we face unpleasant situations and not get too stimulated while dealing with pleasant situations. As the saying goes, when the going gets tough, the tough get going.

One way to prepare for life's challenges is to cultivate a growth mindset. This means approaching obstacles with an open mind and a willingness to learn from mistakes. It also means embracing challenges as opportunities for growth rather than viewing them as setbacks. By doing so, we can develop resilience and become more capable of handling whatever comes our way. Another way to prepare is to build a strong support network. Having people in our lives who we can turn to for guidance and support can make all the difference during difficult times. It's important to cultivate these relationships and to be there for others as well.

This book is an effort to understand life. This will take you through the diverse and complicated human emotions based on my own personal experiences and the experiences of the people around me in various aspects of life. How to embrace life's unpredictable journey by navigating ups and downs, we will hopefully learn towards the end of this book.

1
People and Need of People

We have grown up thinking we need people around us, people to talk to, to share our feelings with, to socialize with, to get rid of our boredom, to help us in a time of need, and multiple other reasons. With this notion being repeatedly fed to us, we think we couldn't survive without friends, family, and relatives.

Let me tell you that's not true.

I have been brought up with a similar mindset. My inherent nature is, however, contradictory. I am not an extrovert person as breaking the ice with someone doesn't naturally come to me. I am more of "You start first then I will talk to you" kind of a person which essentially means I am diffident. When I was young, I would not open until the other person started talking and when I open, I would talk like a gobbledygook, to an extent that I would disclose even the most private matter of my life. This means that I was not sensible but inherently dependent on other people. As a young boy, I focused on making many people as friends so that I always have company, at school, at playground, in the neighborhood and wherever I go and used to think that the more people I know the more I can count on them at the time of need. Over time, I became more convinced that more people would make my life easier, but my own inability always stood in the way. My inherent shyness has never really allowed me to make friends.

Ask yourself:

- Do I need people around me?
- If yes, why do I need people around me?

When I reflect on my life, I gather that I never had a pleasant experience with people.

At my workplace, I made connections with many people for company, initially confused them for friends as I would often share secrets about personal and professional life, but subsequently realized they can't be friends. With maturity and age, I understood that professional colleagues can only be acquaintances owing to fierce rivalry and the mad rat race to prove supremacy for staying ahead of the game. I have paid a heavy price for blabbering and sharing things I should have never discussed. What I didn't understand though was that the necessity of having people in my life was more of my inherent need of dependence. The dependence to gain sympathy, empathy, to validate my opinion when other people feel the same way I feel about a situation, to vent out frustration about anything which is bothering me, satisfying my ego by bringing more people by my side having similar thought process. What I did not realize is that by doing so I was becoming weaker. Having dependence on others is a sign of a weak person. It was the first time I noticed it when there were quarrels back home. To hear a colleague's or friend's opinion on the subject and then respond accordingly, I often discussed even the most trivial of issues with them. We all have a responsibility to the outcome of our actions, but we often influence other people's decisions in this kind of situation and affect their judgment. When I've faced many unpleasant situations at work, this thought of not sharing professional and personal matters with people around me has grown more powerful. On numerous occasions, I have expressed something, yet the message that was conveyed was different. I was always misconstrued, and words were no means to convey my discomfort. I almost always ended up on the wrong side of the fence. This made my conviction to not share my feelings with my colleagues stronger. Even then I am a human and to err is human. I still make mistakes sometimes. Guess, this is called maturity which you can achieve only with age and failures. I have been in those situations many times both on a personal and professional front. Upon reflection, I came to the realization that I would have been better served by not participating in those situations.

For example, when I got an invitation to the birthday party of a friend while I knew if I went there were strong chances of a clash with one specific person and yet I went ahead and attended the party because my friends convinced me and later realized I should not have attended. I have gone against my gut feeling on many occasions, only to regret later.

This helped me to understand:

- You don't need validation for your actions from others.
- You don't need others to tell you what is good for you.
- You know when to withdraw from a conversation.
- You find people both intriguing and exhausting.
- You love being alone but appreciate good company.
- Your energy levels are closely tied to your environment.
- You would rather say what's on your mind than make small talk.
- You enjoy socializing, but always have an escape plan.
- You are selective with your people and your social calendar.
- You know going solo is more important than being with a person you don't like. Certain people drain you, while others energize you.
- Slowly, you start distancing yourself from others. The effect that those people used to have on you is not the same anymore.
- You are an extrovert person, but you like the company of only those people who match your wavelength.

Suddenly, you quit getting swayed by people around you. Now you start to realize that no one can decide about you but yourself. On multiple occasions, I ended up ruining my mood rather than improving it by being involved in something or spending time with someone I could have easily avoided. I frequently realize after those meetings that I shouldn't have been involved.

This taught me that we should not waste our energy on:

- The people who don't support us.
- What others think about us.

- Onesided relationships.
- The people who need us occasionally.
- Solving problems that aren't ours.
- Doing things just to stay distracted.
- Somebody who isn't interested.

Bhagavad Gita says when you bind yourself to a relation and make it a basis of your survival then it becomes a cause of sorrow and suffering.

Being part of a community gives us a sense of belonging. "We need to know that we have a community around us to feel safe, loved and supported. But when we do this continuously, we can forget how to be without the influence of other people. The problem is in the "needing"; needing others to be happy, needing others to fill the missing piece. There are no missing pieces though when you learn to love your own company,"

That's where I started to doubt the fundamental question that challenges my belief of having people around us. As **Aristotle said,** *'Man is a social animal'. He can't survive in isolation.* Therefore, human beings interact with each other daily, having a deep impact on each other's life. This statement is partially true and partially untrue. While we need people around us, with maturity we realize that we don't need them for anything except satisfying our own inherent need of dependence.

Take today's generation as an example. With all the technological disruption happening, there has been a paradigm shift in our behavior patterns. Until a decade back we used to rely on each other's company, but with the advent of the internet, social media platforms, gaming platforms, over the top (OTT) platforms, and all other mediums of vicarious pleasures we don't find the need to have real company. Technology is taking over humans. Playgrounds are replaced by gaming stations, social gatherings are replaced by movie marathons, personal chats are replaced by virtual chats and a lot more is happening on the internet. People are hooked on platforms like reels on Instagram, YouTube videos, TikTok apps and consuming all sorts of random content. These platforms serve us contextual content that suits our mood, personality, likes and dislikes. My son, being a single child and both his parents working without any other company, is heavily dependent on his I-pad for playing games. These interventions have only accentuated what was already imminent.

Increased screentime is leading to a lot of problems like anxiety, depression, sleeplessness, and lack of attention among others. While our health is at risk but more importantly there is a heightened risk of being isolated. The World Health Organization (WHO) has declared loneliness to be a pressing global health threat, with the US surgeon general saying that its mortality effects are equivalent to smoking 15 cigarettes a day. Invariably we are getting trapped in a vicious circle. First, we isolated ourselves, then we became dependent on proxy lifestyle. We no longer need people around us as we are happy in our own virtual world. Even the family we live in no longer matter to us. Alas, it's a sad situation but it's the reality of today's life. The fact that we are so dependent on our phones and proxy lifestyle is a testimony to our inherent nature that we don't need people around us.

Today's reality is different. It's paradoxical. We want to use people and want to be used by some, we want to abuse people and want to be abused by some. We keep chasing people whom we are emotionally dependent on and being chased by people who are emotionally dependent on us. The sooner we know it, the better it is.

When I think of myself how emotionally dependent, I am on my wife and kid, but they are not. Similarly, my wife is emotionally dependent on her parents, but they are not dependent on her. I feel lonely when I don't get emotional support and likewise my wife feels isolated when she doesn't get that support from her parents.

Once we find out what the purpose of every relationship is, we will know how to keep it. And ultimately, it's about the maintenance of boundary between all relationships. To whom we call friends and only meet on weekends are no friends, they are mere acquaintances whose company we like, and we love to have fun with. The relationship we call the most intimate but doesn't give the freedom to express what's on our mind is not a close relationship. Knowing the value of each relationship and setting boundaries will ensure our peace of mind and a long-term association.

The word "alone" has many different connotations. You can be in a solitary confinement or the comfort of your living room and be physically alone. You can go to a concert by yourself and be socially alone, feeling that you can't connect with those around you. Or you can be emotionally alone. When you are emotionally alone, you don't have a person that you connect with on a regular basis, someone who provides emotional support and kindness. You may have friends and family, but the interactions are superficial, and the relationships lack deep connection and understanding. You may even be in a relationship where you don't receive the kind of support you need. (This can be much worse than being single, as someone is taking up the space where your person belongs, preventing someone else from filling the role.) You may be a single parent who has plenty of contact with tiny humans every day but lack the kind of outlet for the daily stresses of parenthood that an adult connection can provide. Or you may be single with no close family and no deep friendships.

As human beings we are hardwired to seek connections with others. For most, it is not by choice that we find ourselves alone — that is, without a person — and for those for whom it is their choice, it is often out of a need to protect oneself from vulnerability. But for those of us who desire connection and are willing to be vulnerable, there are things we can do in the meantime that will help us to lead more fulfilling lives, to stave off loneliness and isolation, and to grow as human beings.

If we have the power to go alone to a restaurant or a movie theatre, then we can do anything in life.

Being in control when living alone means you get to make all the big decisions that directly affect our destiny.

When it comes to what you do, who you socialise with and when you choose to do the things you are passionate about – all of this, and more, is under your control, for you to make decisions upon without judgement, compromise, or justification.

We can choose the right people in our life by following some basic rules. They can be as simple as:

- Losing toxic people.
- Having deep conversations with the right people.
- Staying away from the people who act like a victim in a problem they created.

- The people we allow into our life are contagious so, choosing them wisely and quickly.
- Knowing that the best weight we will ever lose is the weight of other people's opinion of us.
- Being alone will always be better than being with someone who doesn't value who we really are.
- Realizing one day how there are some people who are not meant to be ours. We will have to move on, and the most important thing is to let it go.
- It's better to have one friend who is happy for us, supports our win, encourages our dreams than a bunch of acquittances who are lazy, selfcentered, and jealous of our success.

When I applied these learnings on my life, I felt so light. It was like taking off a 1000 kg weight off my chest. I have no burden of other people's opinion of me, knowing my peace of mind is in my hands and not in the hands of other people. Letting go of the people who don't value me have made a huge difference in my life.

It made my beliefs stronger about having the right people in my life. Upon introspection, I concluded some great ways we can implement to discover peace among ourselves and others:

1. Seek to love, not to control other people:

First, if you want to have inner peace with others, you must understand that you are there to help and to express your love toward others. You are not there to control others.

Trying to control other people and force people to accept your thinking is a sure way to destroy your inner peace. You have to understand that everyone is different, even with the people who are close to you.

If you want people to understand you, you must first understand them from their point of view. When you try to gain too much control in your relationship with other people, conflicts will arise, and the relationship can falter.

2. Practice tolerance:

Tolerance is all you need to create peace between you and others. It will make all the difference when things are going wrong. Tolerance for others is about appreciating the diversity, the many choices in the society, and being willing to live and let others live too.

When things become intense and people started to lose their tolerance, it can lead to depression, discrimination, and violence. Why do you think people fight with each other? They lose their temper because they have lost their tolerance for each other.

3. Walk away:

Sometimes, it is better to just walk away from a tense situation. This often occurs in meetings or gatherings. When two or more people with different opinions try to gain control of the situation, conflicts can occur and people may go into the argument mode, which eventually may turn into a serious quarrel.

Never let this happen by choosing to walk away. You have to understand that when you are angry or trying to win over a conversation, you will lose your sense and all you do is to argue to let the other party knows that you are right.

Therefore, choose to walk away. Take a break and go and get something to eat. When you change your state, your thinking will change. And suddenly, you will discover new solutions and start to understand what other people are trying to say. This happens because you are at peace with yourself.

4. Live in the moment:

One of the most effective ways to live in peace within you and with others is to learn to live in the moment. When you are living in the moment, you are in a state of mindfulness where you are not your thoughts, but rather, you become the observer and see how your thoughts flow.

This is a higher self-awareness state that a lot of people try to achieve. When you are living in the moment, you can see the big picture clearly and you are able to gain new perspectives on problems and obstacles you face in life.

5. Do not compare yourself to others:

Do you know that the fastest way to lose your peace and joy is to mindlessly compare yourself with other people? While it is true that comparison can create competition and improvement, but most people are just mindlessly comparing everything in their lives with others.

When they see their friends driving a new car, they want one too. When they see their friends travel overseas, they want to do the same as well. It is alright to compare, but you must positively compare so that you can improve and live a better life, and not compare for the sake of comparing.

6. Accept other people just the way they are:

This is a powerful way to find peace within you and others. Remember, you cannot change others and there is no way you can make other people be and act just like you.

Everyone is unique and everyone has their own way of thinking. You just need to accept them the way they are. When you try to change other people, you will end up losing your inner peace and go into an argument because people will find that you are trying to violate their "rules" and characters.

Instead of fighting over changing people, choose to accept them. Understand them from their standpoint and accept them as who they are.

7. Take full responsibility for whatever happens in your life:

One of the key factors to achieving amazing success in life is to take full responsibility for whatever that is happening in your life. When you take the responsibility, you are in control. And when you are in control, you will be at peace because you understand it very well that thing occurs that way because of your choice.

And when you take the responsibility, you have the power to change. For example, when you fail in your business, you can choose to blame the economy, your client, your employees, or anything. However, if you take responsibility and understand that it is your choice and decision that has led you where you are, you will be in control.

When you are responsible, you are in control, you can change, you can improve, you can do things differently, and more importantly, you will find peace, both within yourself and with others.

Remember, no one can make you feel inferior without your consent. No one can make you feel sad, angry or make you feel bad unless you accept them in the first place. Hence, take responsibility for your life and you will find peace.

Coming back to the point of the need to have people around us. My conclusion is 'YES'. We need people in our lives, but we can ensure our peace of mind by following some simple rules.

We should:

- Stop taking things personally.
- Stop being judgmental.
- Be more tolerant.
- Be more patient.
- Stop gossiping.

As per Bhagavat we should practise tolerance and forgiveness. Tolerance teaches us to face the hardships of life with equanimity and to desist from using force even when provoked. Forgiveness helps us pardon injustice and overcome the feelings of animosity. Both these qualities are crucial to maintain and nurture relationships, develop feelings of empathy and love, and overcome divisive thoughts.

Our actions and nature determine whether or not we have people in our lives. What matters is that we should know how to live with or without people.

My Guru taught me that the first and most important thing we need to know is that we are souls and not the body. When we accept this, then the relationship with our mother, father, brother, sister, wife, or the world would have no value for us because we are not the body; these people are related to our bodies.

None of our relations in this world know where our welfare lies, so how can they benefit us? How can a blind man show the path to another blind man? It's such a simple fact. Our relationship with God is from eternity and will exist forever. We are a fraction of Him. The Vedas say, "We are a part of Him and are his sons also. and only He is our everything." It says "only" not 'also.'

Hence, we should treat all relationships with equanimity and focus on discharging our basic duties towards everyone. Like raising a child and making him capable to lead a life on his own, providing for family, wife etc. It's our Dharma. Beyond Dharma we should not have any attachment towards anyone.

We have two choices:
1.Be alone or
2.Be with someone.

Being in a society we need people around us, but some appreciate, some criticize. Finding someone who appreciates every smallest thing we do in life is very hard to find but if we have, we will cherish life to the fullest. Being alone can be a choice but it may make us depressed which is something we all hate to see for ourselves. We all need someone to talk to and share our feelings with. It's our choice to decide who that person is. It could be another human being or God our true guide.

Remember God is our eternal friend and will never leave us.

"A person can rise through the efforts of his own mind; or draw himself down, in the same manner. Because each person is his own Friend and Enemy." – Bhagvad Gita

In the next chapter we will discuss Anger and how to deal with anger issues which is a very important factor in interpersonal relationships.

2

Anger

- I hate when I see people lying on my face, it makes me angry all the time.
- I'm being called an angry young man by friends and family because I lose my temper easily.
- I felt so angry after my wife cancelled the plan to watch a movie at the last minute.
- I get amazingly irate when I don't get food on my plate as I couldn't control my starvation.
- I screamed at my friend on the cricket field for missing the fielding and giving away unnecessary runs.
- I lost my composure at home, shouting at my brother for proving I'm right, and he's wrong.
- I've got a lot of expectations from my wife, but she doesn't live up to them, so I get angry and don't want to talk to her.
- I lost my temper while we were discussing the regular business of our office and shouted at a colleague above his voice in order to substantiate what I was saying.
- I was frustrated for having an argument with my boss and vented out the frustration on my wife for a very silly issue.
- I just lost my cool after eating a bland vegetable cooked by my maid and howled at her for cooking such insipid food.
- My son's complaint is that his teacher has been shouting at class, and the kids have been subjected to unremittingly vulgar language from him.
- I witnessed two people arguing in the middle of the road due to an accident caused by one of them because of rash driving and blocking all traffic.

- I came back home after a long hectic day and found out my son didn't score good marks in maths even after so much of practice, so I screamed at him.
- Sometimes, when I can't control a situation and when someone is not listening to me, I feel like slapping that person and control him through physical dominance.
- I've seen two of my close friends in a nasty argument on something ridiculous, and it was so unpleasant that we were forced to leave the scene.
- A beggar walked up to my car in front of the traffic light this morning. He'd been begging for the money all along. The sight was so extreme that I couldn't bear it anymore and passed it on to him.
- The way my boss acts, it's very erratic. He's set up a toxic culture in the office. Every now and then he uses his high pitch voice to deliver feedback or use comments below the belt, insulting those who work for him.
- Two friends of mine were sitting and talking about politics at a social gathering the weekend, and they had differing views on their ideologies. The debate turned to a point of disagreement, and all the more so when it boiled down to fighting.

We all witness so many scenes of anger around us. People getting angry for the silliest of reasons and losing their temper. In all the above scenarios, I ordinarily lose my self-control and feel awful after the outrage dies down. I realized that other individuals and I might have responded in an unexpected way in these circumstances in case outrage had not taken over us. Over the years, my anger has caused so much damage to my reputation. It's made a recognition that I am touchy and effortlessly incited. I have been manipulated, misused, and scoffed at.

Imagine if I remained calm in all these situations, what would have been the outcome.

- Have I been a better person? Or
- Have I been a worse person?

We all know the answer. This is what usually outrage does to all of us. We all agree anger is not a positive sentiment. It prevents the ability to think properly. Anger, undoubtedly, is one of the major reasons of human suffering. When one loses his temper, he loses his reasoning too and ends up doing things which he repents later. Such an irrational behaviour creates problems not only for the person concerned but also for others around him.

As a young professional, I used to have lot of arguments in office. During those arguments, I mostly lost my temper. It didn't affect anyone except me. It disturbed my peace of mind and I used to carry it at home which affected the atmosphere at home. I always repented it later.

It made me think:

- Why did I get angry at the first place?
- Could I have avoided it?

Let us understand why we get angry?

Cause of Anger

As per the spiritual Bhagavad Gita (2.62):
- It all starts from a stimulus, i.e., a sense object (anything used as enjoyment or satisfaction of our senses).
- While contemplating on that, the person develops attachment for it.
- From that attachment, lust or craving originates as we wish to enjoy that again and again.
- When this craving is not fulfilled, anger arises.

Let's understand with the help of a story:

Sunda and Upasunda were two demon brothers. They were very powerful and ruled over the world. But sexual infatuation caused their downfall. Legend has it that Sunda and Upasunda got the boon that they will never be defeated by Devas, Demons or humans or animals if they fought together.

The prosperity of their clan and family depended on the unity among the two brothers.

Together they drove out Devas from heaven. They defeated Indra and ruled the three worlds. They made Amaravati, the capital of Devas, as their new home.

Devas realized that it was impossible to defeat Sunda and Upasunda through force. So, they resorted to trickery.

Tilottama, one of the most beautiful Apsaras in heaven, was deputed for the job. She seduced the two brothers. The moment the brothers saw Tilottama, they lost their senses and wanted to make her their wife.

Tilottama agreed to become the wife of the strongest among Sunda and Upasunda.

Soon argument ensued among the two brothers as to who among them was the strongest.

Soon argument turned into fight. Both matched each in strength and ended up killing each other before Tilottama.

Moral of the story: Anger is an extremely dangerous sentiment which can cause irreparable damage.

This constant desire towards materialistic pleasures and making it a source of happiness and inability to possess it has become a cause of anger in us. When one desire gets fulfilled, we instantly desire for another and after fulfilment another and this madness never stops. When one comes in contact with any object (which one sees, hears, or tastes etc.), one develops an attachment (a like or dislike) for it. From such like or dislike develops a desire to possess or to get rid of that object. Non-fulfilment of desire breeds' anger. Anger leads to clouding of judgement, and impairment of judgement results in bewilderment of memory (one forgets as to what is right and what is wrong). When the memory is bewildered, intelligence (the wisdom) is lost. Instead of using his discrimination diligently, one flows with the stream of emotions. As a result, one falls into degradation. He is ultimately ruined.

Effects of Anger

In Bhagavad Gita (2.63), Lord Krishna says:
- Anger leads to complete delusion or loss of judgment.
- From delusion, memory is bewildered.
- When this happens, intelligence gets lost.
- And the person falls in this chain of events.

When we act in anger, *krodha vegam*, we do things that we regret later. In Bhagavad Gita (16.21), anger is considered a gateway to hell, and we are asked to avoid it to avoid suffering. Anything in excess causes harm and the same is the case with anger.

Let's understand with the help of a story:

A saint used to go door to door for alms. One day he reached house a rich man of village to beg for alms. Saint brought some grains and gave them to saint as alms.

After giving alms, Rich man said, "Maharaj I want to ask a question. "

Saint replied, "Sure..."

Rich man Said, "I want to know why people fight?"

Listening to this, saint remained silent for some time and then replied in loud voice, "I have come here to take alms, I have not come here to answer your silly questions..."

Hearing this, Rich man got very angry and lost control of himself and started shouting at saint saying, "What's this behaviour? I just gave you alms and yet you are answering me like this..."

Rich man said many things to saint in anger. Saint was standing there listening to him silently and did not say a word when Seth was shouting.

After some time, when Rich man calmed down, then Saint said to him, "Brother as soon as I responded to you badly, you got angry. In anger you started shouting at me. If I had also become angry at that time, then there would have been a big fight between us.

Anger is the cause of every quarrel and peace can end every dispute. If we don't get angry then there will be no fight.

"Learning: Whether at home, family, or workplace, we should remain calm. Even if someone is getting angry, we should answer calmly. As soon as we lose our calm and get angry, even small things can do big harm.

Does it happen to you as well?

- How do you react?
- What do you think would have happened if you reacted differently?

We all know that most of the time our reactions cause problems for us. Life is 10% of what happens to you and 90% of how you react. This made me to further think about how to control my anger. Here is what I think we should do.

Ways to Control Anger:

Let's first read a story to understand:

Once upon a time there was a billionaire. He went to a saint and said, "My health condition is very bad. I always have headache; I can't digest my food and I always feel sleepy. I don't know the solution of this problem. My wife is a dumbest girl. She is very lazy. And all my servants are thief. They don't do their job in right time. My brother doesn't understand me. He does whatever he likes to do. That's why I am angry all the time. Please tell me any solution". The saint said, "Show me your hand". The man showed his hand. The saint said, "I am very sorry, I can't do anything." The man shouted, "Please tell me anything, I don't know what to do". After this the saint said you have only 10 days to live. Listening this the billionaire got shocked. The billionaire went his home back. On ninth day he returned to the saint and started explaining his experience of these days. The saint asked, "Were you angry in these 9 days"? The billionaire answered, "No".

This is the main thing about life. When we know our end is coming, we become productive and don't complain anything. We forget negative emotions like anger and fulfil our duties. The same thing is said in Bhagavad Gita. The one who is born will surely die. And **Steve jobs** has also said, remembering that one will die soon is the most important tool that has helped him to take big choices in life. Because all the external expectations, all pride, all fear of embarrassment or anger will fall in front of death.

When I reflected on my behaviour, I realized life is too short to be angry all the time and with everyone.

By understanding the cause and effects, we can conclude that we can control anger by:

- Instilling better qualities.
- Differentiating between needs and desires.
- Taking help from God, meditating, and praying.
- Pausing for a while and thinking of the consequences of anger.
- Not being too attached to people, objects, power, money, etc.
- Consciously reducing and changing our endless material desires.
- Controlling the mind by making it our best friend (Bhagwat Geeta 6.6)
- Reading Bhagavata and other spiritual books that remind us of the right path.
- Having a role model to seek inspiration from and a mentor who can train and guide us.
- Putting good inputs (hearing, listening, reading, watching the right content) in mind to get better outputs (knowledge, bliss, peace, satisfaction).
- Staying away from addictions and bad habits.

Below are few verses from Bhagwat Gita which explain about anger:

"dhyayato visayan pumsah sangas tesupajayate
sangat sanjayate kamah kamat krodho 'bhijayate" **(Bhagwat Gita: Chapter Two verse 62)**

"Sri Krishna said: O Arjuna, one develops attachment for the sense objects by thinking about the sense objects. Desire for sense objects comes from attachment to them, and anger comes from unfulfilled desires."

"krodhad bhavati sammohah
sammohat smriti-vibhramah
smriti-bhramsad buddhi-naso
buddhi-nasat pranasyati" **(Bhagwat Gita: Chapter Two verse 63)**

"Sri Krishna said: O Arjuna, those who are free from anger and all material desires, who are self-realized, self-disciplined and constantly endeavouring for perfection, are assured of liberation in the God in the very near future."

"dambho darpo 'bhimanas cha
krodhah parusyam eva cha
ajnanam chabhijatasya
partha sampadam asurim" **(Bhagwat Gita: Chapter Sixteen verse 4)**

"Sri Krishna said: O Arjuna, Pride, arrogance, conceit, anger, harshness and ignorance—these qualities belong to those people who are of demoniac nature."

These advice by Krishna is so relevant and scientific in today's context.

When I reflected upon my behaviour, I realized the reasons I get angry most of the times is because of unfulfilled desires. The desire to control people around me, possess material things, grow in life, achieve small and big targets set for myself et al. The inability to fulfil my desires lead to anger.

After reading this, I asked myself:

- How can I deal with anger?
- Is there a way I cannot get angry in inevitable situations?

That reminded me of Guru's teachings. My Guru taught me to look at Anger in two different ways:

1. Deal with anger in a similar way we get angry at a child.

We scold kids for various reasons, when they don't finish the food and milk, not completing their homework, not carrying on in an endorsed or suitable way craved by us. When we reprimand them, the anger directed at kids is not real. We usually create an aura of anger whilst we are not angry from inside. We shout at them to show our anger. It is only to instil fear in them to make them understand the difference between good and bad. This helps in making them a better human being. We can follow the same approach in life. We should maintain a calm composure inside and address the issue and forget about it.

2. Think of yourself like a child always.

A child doesn't take any anger directed at them personally and drag it beyond a point. When we scold a child, they will cry instantly and after a while they will act normally and come to us with the same love and affection. Any amount of anger doesn't change their feeling towards us (This obviously doesn't include exceptional cases where adults abuse the kids. This is in reference to the normal parenting by many folks) If we think of ourselves like a child and stop getting bothered by emotions regardless of how negative, they are, we will never get angry because we would stop taking anything personally and emotionally. The moment we stop taking anything personally, we will observe a huge change inside us. It will change our outlook towards everything. There may be a world of storm around us, but we can choose to remain unperturbed and composed. This is the power of a childlike behaviour. No external factors could affect us.

We all try to control the environment around us, the people, and the situations. We would be happier if we stop controlling the external factors and focus on things within our control.

Here is another story, Krishna's Story: Laugh at your anger!!!

Once, Krishna went on a long journey with Satyaki. Because they failed to reach their destination by sunset, they were forced to sleep in the forest.

Krishna asked Satyaki to keep watch for the first half of the night, and then He would watch for the second half. After making this request, Krishna went to rest on a bed of twigs, which was covered with a chadar (light blanket).

As Satyaki kept watch he suddenly saw a belligerent demon approaching. The demon addressed him in a hoarse voice.

"Listen. I'm very hungry. If you allow me to overwhelm your sleeping friend and eat Him, I will spare your life. Otherwise, I will first kill you, and then afterward fill my belly with both of you."

Satyaki was angered at this unethical proposal, drew his sword, and began to fight the demon. But the demon was stronger.

As the night progressed, and as is the way with these types of demons, he became larger and more powerful. Finally, the demon pushed Satyaki to the ground. As Satyaki waited for the death blow, he closed his eyes in naked terror.

But nothing happened. After some time, he opened his eyes only to find that the demon had mysteriously disappeared.

"Maybe the demon was only an illusion," Satyaki thought. "In this part of the forest, such illusions are common.

" After some time, he woke Krishna as they had agreed, and without mentioning the demon, went to sleep.

The next morning, when Satyaki awoke and the sun was shining, he remembered what he thought was a nightmare and told Lord Krishna about His dream.

"Oh," said Krishna, "you saw a demon and then he disappeared? Is it this one?"

With these words, Lord Krishna pulled out a small demon from His waistcloth that looked exactly like the demon Satyaki had fought during his watch in the night.

Then Krishna became grave.

"Listen carefully, Satyaki. – This is your anger. The moment you gave it attention, it grew stronger. Never identify with it. Just look at it, understanding that you are not identical with it, and eventually it will disappear."

Anger is a demon inside us. It comes out when provoked and shows our ugly side to the world. If we work on it consciously, it may be addressed permanently.

Think of ways to calm yourself. Here is what I think we should do:

- Walk : Walking helps clear your mind. It offers you a different perspective.
- Indulge : Take a day off to spend a whole day doing exactly what you want.
- Be Generous : Give something to a total stranger. Acts of giving makes us warm and fuzzy inside.
- Sit in a coffee shop or a busy street and soak up your surroundings. You don't have to talk to people.
- Educate yourself : Research what is it you are experiencing. Arm yourself with knowledge and the resources to tackle the problems head-on.
- Preparation : Write the day's to-do list the evening before.
- Strengths : Write down a list of 20 of your strengths.
- Keep going forward : Keep taking small steps, no matter what. Being stagnant doesn't serve you.
- Re-visit an old hobby : If you don't have one, create one.
- Prioritize : Decide what's important right now. Say no to extra obligations.
- Sleep : Get enough rest. Sleep 7-9 hours each night.
- Be silly : Do something that you did as a child. Don't take life too seriously.
- Cry : Release all that emotion. You will feel better.
- Check your self-talk : Negative self-talk doesn't serve you.
- Journal : Develop a habit of journalizing. This will help free your mind.
- Remind yourself that life is a journey. Remember that what you are going through is temporary, it will pass.

As per my Guru, we should get angry on the anger – Why did we get angry? Each time we get angry, we should introspect and think of the damage it does to us. When it gets repeated, we should be angry again and introspect. With each passing time it will mitigate. One day we will master the art of not getting angry.

He taught me to get angry on the right desire. What is the right desire? The right desire is following the path of spirituality. We ought to be irate with ourselves for superfluously squandering our feelings on common issues and not needing to be near to God. Anger can't solve anything when we have nothing in our control. We ought to figure and be angry with ourselves for not following the righteous path and the path for salvation.

As per my Guru's teaching's, we should not burst into anger when someone commits a mistake. Instead, we should try to solve things amicably and nip any problem in the bud. The fire of anger should be extinguished at the beginning itself, and we should not let it grow into a conflagration.

The next time you get angry introspect, it affects your health and peace of mind. Think of the reason why you are getting angry and is it worth it?

"Delusion arises from Anger. The mind is bewildered by delusion. Reasoning is destroyed when the mind becomes bewildered. One falls down when reason is destroyed." – Bhagvad Gita

In the next chapter we will discuss about friends and friendships which is important to choose the right people in our life.

3
Friends and Friendship

I once believed in friends and friendship. I believed that friendship is the purest relationship which transcend all boundaries of religion, caste, financial status, social status, and any other form of mental barrier. But that has changed now.

I don't feel like talking to my friends, I don't have any friends either. It's not that I had a lot of friends always, but whatever little group of friends I had, I have distanced myself from them. The prospect of meeting my friends don't excite me, their company don't make me happy. If my friends reach-out to me, I will talk to them and meet them otherwise I will not contact them. Seldom do I call and message them and whenever I do, it will be for some work.

The connection with friends is one which is always with the heart and that connection is now broken. Our heart doesn't want to trust anyone anymore, it has become calculative. It works like a transaction or a deal, what is in it for me? What will we get out of the friendship and what does our friends want from us?

- Ah I see He doesn't have anyone to talk to today, and that's why he's thinking about me.
- I think she is feeling alone tonight, so she wants to share her feelings with me. She is so selfish she only thinks of me when she feels alone.
- Well, I see she must be calling to borrow money from me…No no she wants some other favour but there is something she wants from me. She can't call me without any reason.

- If I meet with him today, he's going to waste my time. I could've used my time for something more important instead of wasting it on him.

Such thoughts never crossed our minds when we were kids. In the past, we would spend countless hours talking with the same group of friends every day. Back then it was the only thing we used to look forward to, if a day goes by without meeting a friend it felt like something is missing, something is incomplete, a sense of vacuum would creep inside us. There were no expectations, no calculations, no conditions. Everything was simple, if we wanted to meet our friends, we will meet them come what may. We would come up with silly excuses at home to meet our friends. Back then we will talk about everything and anything under the sun, and no one felt bored or disinterested and we never thought of it as a waste of time. We had no money but a heart full of compassion. We would spend whatever little money we had gladly on our friends. It wasn't the money that concerned us, not the financial status that made any difference, not the IQ level we looked for, it was sheer pleasure of our friends' company which was enough for the day to end on a good note and a beautiful next day to hope for.

Alas! we are not the same people anymore. The burden of responsibilities, the endless race for survival, the madness to run after success and money, the constant endeavour of judging others, the obsession to prove other's wrong and us right has taken away the real pleasures in life. Life is not the same anymore. Now we look for reasons to meet friends. Most of us meet on weekends to have fun. Those whom we call friends are mere acquaintances. We don't know them so well. The only purpose of our meetings is to talk about trivial things. The objective is to unwind ourselves through temporary pleasures. Meeting friends is secondary and having fun is primary. Are we only communicating with our so-called friends on weekdays when it comes to weekend plans? We have confined our friendships to weekends fun, special occasions like birthdays, anniversaries, and personal milestones. When was the last time we met our friends without a plan? How often do we speak to our real friends with whom we can talk about anything and everything? We don't share our emotions, life problems, and good and bad things with our weekend friends. Infact we are scared to share anything. Sharing good news makes us feel insecure about its potential to have a negative impact on themand sharing bad news will accentuate our problems. They are more our gossip buddies. This is the harsh reality of today. We have confined ourselves to a shell.

Sometimes, whom we consider our friends backstab us. They don't value our emotions, disregard our privacy, and breach our trust. It is as if enemies were better than friends. All this happens because we have no moral values, and we don't think beyond ourselves and our interests.

Ask yourself:

- Do I have friends?
- Do I have friends who I can count on when I need them?
- Can my friends count on me when they need me?

How many friends do we have that are reliable and dependable and that we can count on when we need them and vice versa?. we all need someone for emotional, mental, and physical wellbeing. In today's fast paced life, we are so busy to take some time out to check-up on a friend every now and then. We have ample time to browse social media platforms like Facebook, Instagram and WhatsApp and make thousands of friends there, but no time to speak with an old friend occasionally. The faker we are, the bigger our circle will be. The realer we are, the smaller our circle will be. It's a well-known fact. We boast of having a huge community of friends and followers on social media platforms, but we hardly talk to any of them. While our online community keeps growing bigger and bigger our real friends keep getting fewer and fewer. Technology has made us slaves of our own desires. We are drifting away from the real pleasures of life. It's difficult to find true friendship. But who is to be blamed for this? All of us are to be blamed. We have forgotten the true virtues of friendship. We confuse it with selfishness, expectations, temporary pleasures, fun and show off. We make friends to make a statement about our social circle. Someone we can flaunt like clothes. The same friends are not available when we need them for a family emergency, personal exigency, financial help, emotional and physical support. We are on our own. We are so lonely, deep down and we all know it. The more we are moving towards digital economy and modern culture, the more we are embracing solitude.

In today's fast paced and stressed life, there are so many occasions when I feel low due to high work pressure, job related stress, financial problems, health problems, strain in relations and I need someone to share my feeling with, but many a times I don't find that one friend with whom I can share everything without the fear of being judged.

Then I read so much about friendships in our ancient religious books which made me question my behaviour.

- Is it me who is wrong? or
- Is it others?

We can learn a lot about friendships from our ancient religion.

Here are four exemplary stories of friendship from the Bhagavata:

1. Krishna- Friends with children of cowherds:

Krishna though a prince but spent his childhood playing with children of cow herds. He used to have so much fun and frolic with them. One, very well-known pranks that he indulged with his friends was to climb on top of trees and with sling shots break clay pots filled with water carried by womenfolk of the village. The other one was to enter houses with children and steal curd and butter from pots. Infact, it became so popular that even today to commemorate his birthday, pots of curd are suspended at high altitudes and competitions are announced wherein group that can reach till that pot and break it, are declared winners, and are awarded. There are management lessons on teamwork too drawn out of this practice. HIS acts of friendship of-course were just not restricted only to pranks and fun. To protect his friends in difficulty or danger, he never thought twice even if it meant putting HIS own life at risk. Here's a brief recount of the incident. A huge poisonous snake once got into the river Yamuna. The snake had terrorized the entire village. One day while Krishna and his friends were playing ball on the banks of this river Yamuna, the ball mistakenly fell into the river. Without asking any other friend to go and get the ball which HE could have easily done, HE dived into the river, knowing very well that the poisonous snake could kill him. As is known to all, HE returned not just with the ball but also fought and killed the snake.

2. Krishna-Friend of Sudama:

One very unique practice in ancient India was to send children to Gurukul like boarding schools of today. The difference was the Gurukuls used to be nestled in forests and managed by Guru or teacher. Children from all walks of life were students enrolled on basis of merit only and no divide of rich or poor. Children there were taught to be independent and acquired real knowledge. Krishna in HIS gurukul made friends with Sudama who was from a very humble background. Years after they were grown up and not seen each other for years, once when Sudama was in dire need to money, his wife who had heard stories of his friendship with Krishna, asked him to approach Krishna for help. Sudama, very hesitantly went to the huge palace not sure if Krishna would remember him still let alone allowing him to get inside the gates. But, lo and behold moment Krishna was informed by guards that Sudama was at the gate seeking permission to see HIM, Krishna ran to welcome him at the gate. Not only that, as per tradition, he made Sudama sit and to the surprise of everyone present including Sudama, HE washed his feet and wiped it as a gesture of hospitality. This teaches us a very powerful lesson on importance of 'humility'. Greatness is attained through the path of 'humility' and never through 'arrogance'. On hearing about the poor financial situation of Sudama, HE immediately offered bags of gold coins. Sudama's joy knew no bounds. This is 'Selflessness' in friendship. It's about giving wholeheartedly without expecting a return.

3. Krishna- Friend of Arjun:

Arjun considered Krishna as his Friend and Guide. In the defining battle of Kurukshetra, Arjun requested Krishna to be his charioteer to direct the horses which was infact symbolic of mind too. Horses in chariot like our mind if not directed well will go in all directions and never reach its goal. Krishna without any hesitation became his charioteer. Infact, just when the battle was about to begin, Arjun seeing his near and dear ones standing against him became emotionally weak and wanted to give up and not fight. At that moment Krishna, his friend played the role of a great guide. He explained to him his duty and about righteousness, all of which is captured in holy book of Gita. We all know after which Arjuna rose and fought and won.

4. Krishna and Radha:

These are the subjects of numerous songs often describing romantic relationship between them. But there was more than the romantic feeling between them. While Krishna was a smart boy, Radha was wise. She believed in following the traditions as they were. Whenever Krishna made mistakes, she was the one to correct him. For example, when Krishna killed a bull, Radha was enraged. She told him to bathe in the major rivers of the world to eliminate his sins. Krishna is believed to have brought water from Yamuna, Ganga, Sindhu, and Saraswati into two ponds now known as Radha Kunda and Shyam Kunda. In that sense, though Radha and Krishna's friendship is not much told in stories, they had deep regard for each other.

The essence of these tales is that we shouldn't expect anything out of our friendship. If we're truly friends, then a friend will know what we need without us sharing our feelings. An example of an ideal friendship, which transcends worldly attachments, is the bond between Krishna and Arjun. It teaches us that in trusting relationships, we have to seek the guidance of God and look for strength and inspiration. Krishna's role as a divine guide and Arjun's unwavering trust in him are central to their extraordinary relationship.

What exactly is Friendship?

Friendship is a state of enduring affection, esteem, intimacy, and trust between two people. In all cultures, friendships are important relationships throughout a person's life span.

Friendship is generally characterized by five defining features:

1. It is a dyadic relationship, meaning that it involves a series of interactions between two individuals known to each other.
2. It is recognized by both members of the relationship and is characterized by a bond or tie of reciprocated affection.
3. It is not obligatory; two individuals choose to form a friendship with each other. In Western societies, friendships are one of the least prescribed close relationships, with no formal duties or legal obligations to one another.
4. It is typically egalitarian in nature. Unlike parent-child relationships, for instance, everyone in a friendship has about the same amount of power or authority in the relationship.
5. It is almost always characterized by companionship and shared activities.

One of the primary goals and motivations of friendship is companionship. In addition, adolescent and adult friendships often perform other functions, such as serving as sources of emotional support and providing opportunities for self-disclosure and intimacy.

Availability and quality of intimacy are associated with well-being for men and women alike. Studies showed that men who reported that they felt a lack of emotional support from their wives were far more likely to experience heart attacks. Several other studies showed that both men and women in relationships rated as high in intimacy were less likely to report symptoms of depression and anxiety than those in relationships rated as low in intimacy.

Good friends are good for your health. Friends can help you celebrate good times and provide support during bad times. Friends prevent isolation and loneliness and give you a chance to offer needed companionship, too.

Friends can also:

- Increase your sense of belonging and purpose.
- Boost your happiness and reduce your stress.
- Improve your self-confidence and self-worth.
- Improve your work-life-balance.
- Help you cope with traumas, such as divorce, serious illness, job loss or the death of a loved one.
- Encourage you to change or avoid unhealthy lifestyle habits, such as excessive drinking or lack of exercise.

This is so true. I have a colleague in my office who still takes out time to meet his friends every day. He has made it a habit. Every day after going back home, he switches off his phone and steps out, gets into his car and drives. Then he goes to pick-up a neighbourhood friend, and both play tennis at a nearby club. After sweating in tennis for an hour, he goes to an old restaurant from his childhood days where he meets his other friends, drink tea and spend time for an hour together. They discuss the day's routine, what went well and what did not go well for each of them and together they try to find a solution for anyone who is in problem. Comes back home afterwards and spend time with his family. This is his daily routine after office. He has disconnected himself from the vicarious life completely and prefer spending time with his real friends. He is a little awkward in today's context but at least it makes him feel real. When I meet him in the office he glows and looks completely fresh. His energy levels are better than others, his outlook towards life is positive and he spreads the positivity in office. I asked him if he shares everything with his friends and if his friends are available for him for any kind of help. Without hesitation he says yes and that he does the same for them. It made me realize friendship is a two-way process. It cannot sustain based on one side effort. He takes out time from his busy schedule to meet his friends and his friends do the same for him. He never cribs because it gives him happiness.

And then I thought about myself where did I go wrong. I pondered and realized we ought to know what to anticipate from a companionship. Here is what I think we ought to anticipate.

What can we expect from friends?

1. **Support During Rough Times:** We all go through rough times with family life, work-life, and many other life events that are thrown our way! Having people to talk to during these times is invaluable— and having that support should be something you expect out of a friendship. In a great friendship, we support our friends through rough times and come to expect that they will do the same for us.

2. **Trust For Each Other:** Trust in, and for, each other is vital in a friendship. We must know that when we ask a friend to keep something to themselves, they will. This expectation of trust should also include trusting your friend to not judge you, gossip about you, or laugh at you when you share your feelings, secrets, dreams, and more.

3. **Respecting Boundaries and Expectations:** Talking to your friends about your expectations can help set healthy friendship boundaries. Once you have set these boundaries, you should expect your friends to respect them.

4. **Openness With Feelings:** It's okay to be annoyed or upset with a friend from time to time. However, you should have the expectation in your

friendship that if you are doing something that upsets your friend—they will come to you to discuss the situation, rather than talk behind your back or grow distant. To foster a solid friendship, we must know our friends feel comfortable coming to us to discuss the tough stuff. If a friendship involves tough conversations, had in a respectful manner, it can even help to bring you closer.

5. **A Genuine Interest in Getting to Know Each Other**: Friendship shouldn't be one sided. One person shouldn't do all the talking and the other, do all the listening. Both parties should have a genuine interest in getting to know each other including each other's past, present and future dreams. By learning more about your friend, you will learn more about their expectations from you as a friend.

6. **Compassion When Mistakes Are Made**: No friendship is perfect. However, we should be cognizant of the mistakes we make in a friendship and give each other grace when we err. Sometimes friends might miss the mark on meeting your expectations, or you may miss the mark on meeting theirs. It's important to show compassion for each other and talk through issues in an understanding manner.

My Guru taught me that friendship is only possible with God, our true benefactor. He is present within us, watching our actions, guiding us towards the right path, warning us against any wrongdoing, and determining our future based on good and bad karma. Despite our abuse and curses towards him, he continues to do all of this without expecting anything in return. He considers it his duty. Developing a bond with God will eliminate the need for any mortal being to be our friend. He will always be present around us and in all the activities, and if we have strong faith in him, he will take care of us. There is no friend better than him.

The power of Friendship in real sense was taught by Krishna. He taught us that Friendship transcends all forms of perceived boundaries. True friendship knows no barrier of rich or poor, male, or female or even for that matter human and animal. Friendship is in-fact all about feelings of trust, sharing of joy or pain, being available in time of need.

Krishna to Arjun, "I envy no one, nor am I partial to anyone. I am equal to all. But whoever renders service unto me in devotion is a Friend is in me and I am also a friend to him." – Bhagvad Gita

Let us forge friendships which are without expectations and more yielding. That way we can make long lasting bonds.

In the next chapter we will discover about greed and how it can destroy our relations.

4

Greed

Greed is one among the six enemies. The other 5 being desire, anger, bondage, pride, and jealousy. Lobha in Sanskrit literally means greed or covetousness.

Greed (lobha) is excessive desire, especially the desire to appropriate what belongs to others against the principles of Hindu Sanatana Dharma. It is a never-ending disease. It is a state of mind that is not satisfied even though it has what it wants.

Sometimes greed tempts people to do immoral, illegal, and unethical (someone which is against Dharma) things in pursuit of earning more wealth, woman, and land. Being unsatisfied even after obtaining the object of desire means that the person is greedy.

The world is full of greed and greedy people. We don't have to go too far to witness it. The seeds of greed are sown in the early childhood days.

- When we inquired for that additional chocolate and our mother denied giving it and afterward taking it from the fridge without our mother knowing around it.
- That toffee that we sneaked stealthily absent from the eyes of the shopkeeper considering our act has not been taken note.
- Welcoming our companions over at that point playing video recreations all day long and not permitting our companions have a turn.
- Our parents ensuring, we get a little extra something then the other kids around us.

Does it ring a bell?
Ask yourself:

- Have I been greedy?
- Have I done something similar in my childhood?

Well, it certainly reminds me of my childhood days. Be it stealing chocolate from the fridge, stealing toffies from the shop, and not giving turn to my friends and a lot more things which I have done.

When I was a kid, my father gifted me a bicycle. I was very happy to have my first cycle and I loved riding it. As I grew old, I saw my friends riding motorcycle. Now I wanted a bike. My father bought a bike. It made me feel on top of the world. I would flaunt the bike to my friends. As I graduated and entered post-graduation, many of my classmates used to shuttle by car. I went back to my father and told him we should think of buying a car now, as we need a bigger vehicle for the family to travel together. My father bought a second-hand car. I quickly learned driving and started driving the car to college. Although, I couldn't afford to take the car to college everyday but at whatever point I may, I would drive to the college. Now I got my first job and a few years down the line got married. Now I bought a first-hand car on mortgage thinking I have a certain status in the society, and I should drive a better car. The car became old after a few years and many of my friends replaced their old cars with newer cars. Now I started considering about replacing my old car with a new car and this never ends. The moment my one desire is fulfilled, I immediately set my mind to the next and it goes on and on. This constant desire to uplift my lifestyle by comparing with others made me greedy.

Ask this question to yourself?

- Am I content with what I have?
- Do I compare myself with others?
- Do I crave to have what others have?

We all know the answers. We all compare our economic condition, social status, and a lot more things with others. The unfulfillment of desires lead to anger and frustration.

Even though most of us try not to, we're all guilty of comparing ourselves to others. We can make comparisons like, "I wish I dressed like so-and-so," or, "I wish I were as rich as them."

This is often unconscious, but it's important to try to train ourselves to stop. While it may motivate us to better ourselves, constantly comparing ourselves to others can lead to negative thoughts.

Let us take an example of a crow story from our Hindu Puranas:

A black crow lived in the forest and was happy and satisfied in its life. But one day it saw a beautiful white swan. "This swan is so white," crow thought, "and I am so black. This swan must be the happiest bird in the world."

Crow expressed its thoughts to the swan. "But" the white swan replied, "I was feeling that I was the happiest bird on earth, but when I saw parrot, which has two colors, now I think the parrot is the happiest bird in the whole world as it is more colorful than me."

The crow then moved towards two coloured parrots. The two-coloured parrot told, "I lived a very happy life, but when I saw a peacock, which has multiple colors on its body, but I have only two colors".

The crow then approached the peacock and saw that many people had gathered to see it.

When all the people left the place, the crow went to the peacock and said: "Dear peacock," the crow said, "you are so beautiful with multiple colors on your body. Every day so many people come to see you. When people see me, they immediately shoo me away. I think you are the happiest bird on the earth."

Hearing these words peacock replied, "I always had the notion that I was the most beautiful and happy bird on the earth, but because of my beauty, I am entrapped in this zoo".

Peacock continued: "I have examined the zoo very carefully, and now I have realized that the crow is the only bird not kept in a zoo and that too in a cage. So, for past few days I have been thinking that if I were a crow, I could be happily roaming everywhere as per my own wish and will."

Moral of the story: This shows the greed within us too. We always make unwanted comparison with others and become sad. Many of us never value what God has given us. Thus, all these leads to the vicious cycle of unhappiness, unsatisfied life, jealously and greed.

Comparing ourselves with others, thinking about how blessed they are and how unlucky we are is a sign of greedy people. Such people can never be happy in life as they would always be jealous of others success and happiness and never be happy with their own success.

Thus, we need to learn the secret of being happy and discard the comparison which leads only to unhappiness, unsatisfied life, jealously, greed etc.

Well greed is not just about comparison. It is much more than comparison.

We see so many people around us fighting on the domestic front, with their blood relatives for material possessions like property, money, and other stuff and not caring about the value of those relations. A brother makes comparisons with another brother on his economic status, social status, possessions, physical attributes, wife, children, job, and everything else. Similarly, a sister making similar comparisons. Even brother comparing with a sister and vice versa. The comparison leads to misunderstandings, misunderstanding lead to scuffles, scuffles lead to mental disturbance which ultimately lead to strain in relationships.

This all starts with the greed to be the best. To attain more wealth, improve economic status, enhance material possessions and so on. In our quest to have everything we don't realize we are fighting with our own blood.

Take the case of speculative income generating sources. Look at the example of stock market. We start to invest with the intention of making profits. We become greedy to earn more income in a short time and mistime our exit strategy which in the long run causes misfortunes. If we followed the right exit strategy timed with the market sentiment, we could comfortably make decent profits and exit.

Similarly look at the corruption at workplace. In our quest to make quick bucks and become rich faster, we adopt unethical practices like taking kickbacks, commission etc. to accumulate more wealth in a short time. The obsession to gather more than needed leads to corrupt practices, eventually bringing disrepute to us. For short term gains we pollute ourselves and knowingly participate in bad deeds.

We cheat family, friends, relatives, colleagues, and whoever we can in our degree of influence to make small gains without knowing the damage it could cause to us. We are so blinded by our greed that it does not once occur to us what are we doing and why are we doing. At first, we think it would help build wealth, but the riches gotten by unfair means and indulgence in bodily pleasures also brings its associated problems and misery in its wake. It looks tempting in the short term but makes our life difficult in the long term. In the end it all comes down to the wealth earned through ethical means. Life is what we make of it.

The basic reason for greed is desire. When our desire for material possession gets fulfilled, our desire to want something more increases which results in greed. When the desire doesn't get fulfilled, we become unsatisfied which results in anger. The more desires we create the greedier we become. The less we desire the less greedy we are.

Let's understand this with the story of 'The 99 Club.'

Once upon a time, there was a King who, despite his luxurious lifestyle, was unhappy. One day, he noticed a servant who was happily singing.

The King asked, "What makes you so happy?"

The servant replied, "Your Majesty, I don't have needs. I am happy with a roof over my head and warm food for my stomach."

Not satisfied with the answer, the King sought the advice of his advisor, who said, "Your Majesty, the servant has not passed the 99 Club."

"What exactly is that?" the King inquired.

"Your Majesty, place ninety-nine gold coins in a bag and leave it at his doorstep. I will then explain what the 99 Club is."

The King immediately ordered his people to do it. When the servant found and opened the bag, he jumped with joy and began to count the coins. When he counted ninety-nine gold coins, he wondered, "There must be a hundred. Where is the last one?"

He looked everywhere but in vain. Finally, exhausted, he decided to work harder than ever to earn that last gold coin.

He started overworking and differed from the happy servant who once sang in the palace. Witnessing this drastic transformation, the King asked the advisor what he did to the happy servant.

"Your Majesty, he has now officially joined the 99 Club," the advisor said, "This is a club of people who have enough to be happy but are never content. They are always unhappy about that extra one they do not have."

Does that mean that aiming for one more gold coin is wrong? Should we give up everything and live in austerity to be happy?

Not really. Let's meet Arjun, who is wealthy but not in 'the 99 Club.'

Arjun, an entrepreneur, loves comfort and works hard for it by running his own company. He is rich but not a multi-millionaire, and he knows it does not have to be that way. His lifestyle revolves around traveling the world, loving his wife, and sleeping peacefully at night. In short, he is the happiest man that I know of today.

"What's your trick?" I once asked, to which he replied, "I know the thin line between ambition and greed."

"What is that?"

"Purpose! Whatever I do, there is a noble purpose attached to it for everyone's benefit, and I benefit too. I don't look for ways to exploit anyone for my needs. That will only lead to my downfall."

"Why, downfall?"

"Imbalance! Imagine we are given a pot filled with gold coins, some got a bigger pot, and some a smaller pot based on our skillset. We are all satisfied

with whatever we have. If I start stealing gold coins from someone else's smaller pot to fill my bigger pot, won't it cause an imbalance in the ecosystem? That's when the Mahabharat (fight) starts between the survivors and the suppressors."

What Arjun was suggesting about the 'imbalance in the ecosystem' was the crux of the story of Mahabharata. King Dhritarashtra divided the country in two, giving the prosperous nation Hastinapur to his son Duryodhana and a barren land Khandavprastha to his nephew Yudhishthira.

The Pandavas accepted their uncle's offer, worked hard, and thrived by converting Khandavprastha to Indraprastha. Seeing the progress of his cousins, the greedy Duryodhana, conspired the game of dice, which was the turning event in the story that eventually led to the Kurukshetra war.

Before we move to the story of Mahabharata, let's try to understand if greed is indeed unreasonable.

Let me go back to Arjun's story again. Born in a middle-class family, had it not been for his greed for success, he would not be a millionaire today. But he firmly believes that excessive desire is no longer an optimal strategy for growth.

He says, "Greed is a complex and misunderstood emotion. There is creative greed. Creative greed motivates me to be creative and innovative. And there is destructive greed!"

"Destructive greed?"

"Yes, destructive. That comes with envy. It gets destructive when you see others around you with more money, leaving you feeling inadequate. If you see people doing better, and you are inspired and set goals to reach there, then that is not destructive. But if you want what others have because you think you are entitled to success, money without much effort. That's when you get into destructive greed. I call it envy."

So how is envy different from Greed?

When Pandavas were in the jungle, they led a modest lifestyle. The envious Duryodhana enjoyed stories about Pandavas' miseries from his spies.

One day, he desired to flaunt his magnificence before the Pandavas. On the pretext of hunting, he and his cohorts went near the spot where Pandavas were encamped. They partied, made a loud noise, and did everything to taunt the Pandavas.

On a particular day, Duryodhana insulted a band of the Gandharvas tribe in the jungle. The angry Ghandarvas fought against Duryodhana, defeated him, and took him as a prisoner.

When the Pandavas found that Duryodhana had been taken as a prisoner, they fought the Gandharvas. The Pandavas won and compelled the Gandharvas to release the prisoners. Yudhishthira called Duryodhana his brother, and this approach surprised Duryodhana for a second, but his pride was humiliated. He almost killed himself, but for the hope that the day would come when the Pandavas would be avenged, he decided to return to Hastinapur. He never learned from his mistakes. Instead, he became more envious of the Pandavas over the years and did everything to harm them at the cost of harming himself and his clan.

He was envious of his cousins, so much so that he did not care for his destruction if that harmed Pandavas.

Think about yourself. What kind of greed you have? Is it creative greed? Is it destructive greed? Is it greed because of envy?

Once you know the answer, you will know how to address it.

Greed can also be viewed from the law of diminishing marginal utility angle. According to the Law of Diminishing Marginal Utility (DMU), with the consumption of more and more units of a commodity, the utility obtained from each successive unit decreases. This law explains a significant relationship between utility and the quantity of a commodity that is consumed. This can be better understood by using the example mentioned below:

When we eat food. The first chapatti we eat provides us with great satisfaction. With the second chapatti, we feel less satisfied. As we consume more, we reach a point where we don't need another chapatti and the marginal utility will be zero. After that, if we are forced to eat even one more chapatti, it will lead to disutility. The Law of Diminishing

Marginal Utility causes such a decrease in satisfaction with successive unit consumption. If we apply the same concept to our life, where we accumulate more wealth then needed, we become unhappy as we don't know how to spend that money. We start spending it on wasteful things which fills our head with arrogance and false pride. We start showing off our arrogance through our words and actions. This arrogance which got inside us by way of material supremacy diverts us from the righteous path and we start living in an inflated state of ego. That's where our downfall starts. What goes up comes down.

Greed for material progress is a waste of time. Second, it's an endless chase those who have the wealth of contentment have the greatest wealth of life.

Here is another story from our ancient Puranas:

There was an enlightened laughing saint who lived in a cave, and he constantly used to sing the glories of God.

The saint was always blissful with a cheerful mind, whether there was a storm, rains, cold or hot weather. Before dying the Master left his last testament and will, on a piece of paper in his own handwriting.

His followers and devotees were astounded and surprised that in his last testament he had stated that beneath a nearby stone boulder, he had buried all the gold and money that he had hoarded during his lifetime.

The eager disciples hurriedly got on with the task of digging under the large rock boulder. Deep underneath the rock, they discovered a ragged piece of cloth bundle. Opening the knotted bundle with shaking hands and suspense, they discovered only a lump of dried shit.

There was another scribbled note in the cloth bundle which stated, "If you understood me and my teaching so little that you believed that I ever valued or hoarded wealth in my lifetime, then you are truly heirs to my shit.

Moral of the story: In our greed, we don't even know what we are running after. Is it worth running after? Are we following the herd mentality? What is it that we want to gain from it?

Once we have the answers to all these questions, we will stop chasing unwanted things. We will do ourselves a favour by not wasting our time on things which will yield no result.

Greed is manifested in various other ways.

- Marrying someone for their money rather than for love.
- Making an unfair deal with someone purely because they're desperate.
- Continuing to hoard money when you've got more than you could ever spend.
- Firing long-time employees just to save a few rupees while making billions yourself.
- Being more concerned with your individual happiness than other people's basic needs.
- Prioritizing food, money, or other commodities over your family and their happiness.
- Exploiting natural resources without regard for future generations or the environment.
- Taking all the credit for the success of a group project and not acknowledging the hard work of the rest of your group.
- Inflating the price of life-saving medications just because you know people desperately need them and you want to get rich.
- A person who evades their personal income tax responsibility. While they may say "well, the government was going to waste it anyway", the truth is that everyone needs to contribute their fair share to keep the roads maintained and keep the fire stations open.
- A government official who takes hard-earned taxpayer money and hides it away to use on himself instead of spending them money on improving social services.
- Doing charitable work, not with the intention of helping others but to be blessed with more wealth and accumulating good karma for afterlife. The selflessness is completely absent.

Sri Ramakrishna Paramhansa (1836–1886,) the eminent Hindy mystic of 19th-century India, used stories and parables to portray the core elements of his philosophy. One such story pertains to greed.

Let's read the story to understand better.

The Parable of the Barber and the Seven Jars of Greed

A barber, who was passing under a haunted tree, heard a mysterious voice offer, "Will you accept seven jars full of gold?"

The barber looked around but could see no one. The offer of seven jars of gold, however, roused his cupidity and he cried aloud, "Yes, I shall accept the seven jars."

At once came the reply. "Go home; I have carried the jars to your house."

The barber ran home in hot haste to verify the truth of his strange announcement. And when he entered the house, he saw the jars before him. He opened them and found them all full of gold, except the last one, which was only half-full.

A strong desire now arouses in the mind of the barber to fill the seventh jar also, for without it, his happiness was incomplete.

The barber converted all his ornaments into gold coins and put them into the jar; but the mysterious vessel was as before.

One day he requested the king to increase his pay, saying his income was not sufficient to maintain himself on. Now the barber was a favourite of the king, and as soon as the request was made the king doubled his pay.

All this pay he saved and put into the jar, but the greed jar showed no signs of filling.

At last, he began to live by begging from door to door, and his professional income and the income from begging all went into the insatiable cavity of the mysterious jar.

Months passed, and the condition of the miserable and miserly barber grew worse every day. Seeing his sad plight, the king asked him one day, "When your pay was half of what you now get, you were happy, cheerful, and contented. But with double the pay, I see your morose, careworn, and dejected. What is the matter with you? Have you got 'the seven jars?"

The barber was taken aback by this question and replied, "Your Majesty, who has informed you of this?"

The king replied, "Don't you know that these are the signs of the person to whom the Yaksha consigns the seven jars. He offered me also the same jars, but I asked him whether his money might be spent or was merely to be hoarded. No sooner had I asked this question then the Yaksha ran away without any reply. Don't you know that no one can spend that money? It only brings with it the desire of hoarding. Go at once and return the money."

The wise king's words brought the barber to his senses. He returned to the haunted tree and said, "Take back your gold, O Yaksha."

The Yaksha replied, "All right." When the barber returned home, he found that the seven jars had vanished and mysteriously as they were brought in, and with it had vanished his life-long savings.

Sri Ramakrishna Paramahamsa concluded the story by instilling some wisdom into the hearts and minds of his disciples, "Such is the state of some men in the Kingdom of Heaven. Those who do not understand the difference between real expenditure and real income lose all they have."

Sri Ramakrishna Paramahamsa once said, "Rainwater never stands on high ground, but runs down to the lowest level. So also, the mercy of God remains in the hearts of the lowly but drains off from those of the conceited and the proud.

Sri Sukadeva Goswami said, "Money does not stay in one place. It passes from one hand to another. Ultimately no one can enjoy money, and it remains the property of the Supreme Personality of Godhead." (Srimad-Bhagavatam 5.14.24) Money is God's energy. He created it, He owns it, and He controls it: "Everything animate or inanimate that is within the universe is controlled and owned by the Lord." (Ishopanishad 1).

Krishna determines how much money each of us receives. It may appear accidental that one person is born into wealth and another into poverty, or that one person goes from rags to riches, and another doesn't, but Krishna's law of karma destines these things. Srila Prabhupada says, "Everyone is thinking, 'If I become greedy, I shall get more.' That is not possible. You cannot get a farthing more than what you are destined."

(Lecture, October 3, 1973) And he writes, "It is not possible that simply by endeavors to accumulate more money a person will be able to do so, otherwise almost everyone would be on the same level of wealth. In reality everyone is earning and acquiring according to his predestined karma." (Srimad-Bhagavatam 3.27.8, Purport)

My Guru taught me to be greedy for the true cause.

What is the true cause?

The true cause is to be greedy for seeking the love of your beloved God. In the hopes of attaining material pleasures, we often march physically to religious places, but in our heart, we harbour evil intentions. On some days, our wish is fulfilled, and, in our ignorance, we think it is granted by God. On other days it is not fulfilled, and we think it is not granted by God. When it is fulfilled, we set our sight for another wish. We curse the God when it is not fulfilled. We bribe God by offering material things in lieu of our wish. We make a deal with God that in exchange for his offertory, He will do what we wish. It is not love; it is indeed greed. In our vainglory we forget that we are offering God his own creation. What in the world can we offer to God when everything already belongs to Him.

We have 2 choices:

- To be greedy or
- Not to be greedy.

The choice is ours. We can choose to be greedy for material pleasures or be greedy for the true cause. In the end we have to leave all material possessions here and only our good deeds will go with us.

So, let's not run unnecessarily after what others have & let's try to earn our living by rightful means & do not fall a pray to Greed. Only through continuously contributing and donating to society can we find true rewards that are far greater than the illusion that Greed provides.

Next time let's be greedy for our true cause.

"There are 3 gates to the self-destructive Hell. Lust, Anger and Greed."
– Bhagvad Gita

In the next chapter we will talk about attachment and how to overcome it.

5

Attachment

I know a friend who lost his mother at the age of 9. He was disconsolate as he didn't know what had struck him. As a kid he didn't understand the magnitude of the loss. Without doubts it was a colossal loss. Losing a mother at such an early age is a massive misfortune. He had not imagined a life without mother. Being a young boy, he was strongly dependant on her. She looked after him for everything, right from getting him ready for school, to cooking food and packing lunch for him, to washing his dirty clothes, to ensuring his homework is complete, and putting him off to sleep. It was as if he was incomplete without her. I remember those 12 days (as per Hindu religion) after her passing. Being an elder son, he had completed all the formalities of her last rites. It was so different. He didn't even know how to chant the difficult Sanskrit words and shlokas. Yet he did what had to be done, nonetheless during that emotional state of mind. He has had many weak moments in the school when I would see him crying seeing the mothers of other kids. As he was coming to terms to live a life without a mother, he faced many problems and challenges. He begged and prayed to God to bring his mother back as it was becoming impossible to live without the warmth and care of her love. But his prayer went unanswered. We all know that only thing certain in life is death. He was expecting the impossible. But as they say time is the biggest healer, it filled his wounds, and he got back to living a normal life. A life without a mother which he had not imagined. Soon he learned how to live without her.

During his education days, he lost his maternal grandmother, maternal uncle, maternal aunty, and maternal grandfather. He never saw his paternal grandfather and grandmother as they left him before he was born. Thereafter, he completed his post-graduation and started earning, got married and was blessed with a boy.

He lost his father when his son turned 2 years old. The loss of father was much bigger than a mother's loss. He was so close to his father that he never imagined living a life without him. It broke him and he blamed God for being so unfair and unkind to him. He asked God; why me? Why only I must live without parents. His faith in God was shaken. He was reluctant to accept the reality. He thought God can't be so unfair to someone to deprive them of both the parents. There must be something wrong in his stars. He was so attached to his father that he felt it is impossible to live a life. He was the pillar around whom his whole life revolved. He looked him up for security, both physical and emotional. He was his role model and was a source of inner strength for him. There was so much he learned from him. To a large extent his whole personality shaped around him. In the presence of his father, he was a carefree man who never thought about present and future. But his absence put so much burden on him. From being a son of an officer to becoming a common man. From not worrying about any nature of work to getting stressed for the smallest of work. He felt the burden of world on his shoulders. From thinking about where to start his life again to how to start his life, he was utterly baffled to sort out the mess. I remember him telling me about the advice of his father about running the house independently and saving a penny for the future. Now he was put to test. We all know the psychological resilience as the human ability to "bounce back" after facing adversity, and we are surprised – astonished, even – at the ways in which people can survive, and often thrive, despite their experiences of trauma.

He was once again back on his feet ready to face the life ahead of him. After his father's demise it was time to turn towards his siblings for emotional and physical support. Thankfully, financially he was in good stead. They were supposedly each other's strength, but God wanted to test him more. His father's only asset was the one house he built in his life where he and his brother lived along with their spouses with him during his last days. He wanted to write a bequest in favour of the two of them i.e., his sons, but due to untimely demise it was not executed. As per Hindu law a property is passed to the legal heirs of a father in the absence of a settlement. In this case it was the four of them. His 2 sisters, 1 brother and him. The absence of bequest became a bone of contention and led to dispute within all of them as their extended families were also a part of it. The quarrel continued for seven years after his father's demise and led to a lot of bad blood between them. During this period, he lived the life of a complete wreck, misguided, and misunderstood most of the time. They all decided to sell the house and distribute the share eventually. The attachment that he had for his family turned into hostilities and ultimately indifference.

This is the story of his family. It was like God doesn't want him to have worldly relationships. Some were taken away by God, and others drifted away by circumstances. Many people came into his life and many people left him over the last few years. He bonded with many and was also despised by many. Upon reflection, he realized that whoever he got attached to was taken away from him. It made him a kind of a wreck. He was scared to be attached to anyone for he was insecure that they will be taken away from him and he started looking at everything with despondency.

Then he was introduced to spirituality by me. It changed his perception forever. What he was thinking as an attachment to people was an attachment to his own needs. His whole life ran through him in a flash. From a young boy who lost his mother to a grown-up man who lost his father and everyone else in between. When he was young, he was dependent on his mother for his basic needs. The physical and emotional needs every child is dependent on. He needed his mother for himself and not for her. He was attached to her because she took care of him. Let's put it this way. If his mother had not taken good care of him the way she did and abandoned him, would he still be attached to her? The answer is yes, but if this was the case, he would have different memories of her. If someone took her name in front of him, he would be offended. He is still attached to her being her son in both the cases. In the former, the memories were pleasant, and, in the latter, it was not positive. But, in both the cases he placed himself above her. His attachment to his mother was due to his needs but he was too immature to understand at that time. Same goes for his father. He was attached to his father because he took care of him in his adolescent years and afterwards. The day he lost him, he imagined how it would be living a life alone. Without his father physically, emotionally, and financially, how will he manage his life. The very first thought that came to his mind was about "Him". His life, His future, His family, His needs and so on. What ensued after his father's passing, was also his attachment towards the house to which he was attached to. While in the case of parents they were people, but in the case of house it was a material object. Likewise, he distanced himself from a lot of people because they did not serve his purpose and many people dissociated with him because he stopped serving their purpose. One day as he was reflecting, he realized the same feeling about everyone whom he loved and have been attached to. This made him indifferent towards everyone. He stopped caring about what others think of him.

Constantly thinking on the objects of the senses, one develops attachment to them; and from attachment arise the desire to possess them; and desires give rise to anger (when desires are unfulfilled). (Reference book: Word of God Bhagavad Gita: Chapter 2 verse 62)

Throughout, his life he kept making friends and enemies based on the fulfilment of his desires. When someone behaved as per his expected norms of behaviour, he became attached to them. When someone didn't behave as per his expected norms of behaviour, he detached from them. In both attachment and detachment states, they occupied his mind space. The more useful the worth of someone was, the more he was attached to that person and the less useful the person was the less the attachment was.

Not only my friend but I believe we all are alike when it comes to the people we are attached to.

Think about yourself:

- Am I attached to my loved one's because I love them, or they serve my need?

The more a person serves your need the closer you will be to that person and the lesser a person serves your need the less you will be close to a person.

This has made the definition of attachment clearer to me.

What is attachment?

Attachment can be defined as an emotional bond or strong affinity towards something or someone. It arises from desires, expectations, and the belief that external objects or relationships are essential for our well-being. While attachment itself is not inherently negative, the attachment that leads to dependency and suffering is what the Bhagavad Gita warns against.

Most often the word "attachment" is associated with love. But this is not the complete meaning of the word. Attachment means absorption of the mind. This absorption of the mind can either be through love or even through hate. Thus, whether it be through love or even through hate. Thus, whether it be through feelings of love or even through hate, or in any other way, the absorption of the mind in all cases is referred to as attachment. When there is neither attachment through love nor attachment through hate, that state is referred to as detachment or non-attachment.

Detachment is living in the hustle and bustle of the world without feelings of friendship or enmity towards anyone.

When the mind is free from both attachment and aversion and is absorbed in devotion, one receives the grace of God. Aversion is nothing but negative attachment. Just as in attachment the object of attachment repeatedly comes to one's mind, similarly in aversion the object of hatred keeps popping up in mind. One who controls the mind and is free from attachment and aversion, even while using the objects of the senses, attains the Grace of God.

When Krishna slaughtered them, it was what happened to Kansa & *Shishupala. From the bottom of their heart, they hated Krishna, so absorbed in their hatred that they could see him in everything. And in the course of sleeping, eating, bathing, walking and every other activity. After killing them, Krishna has given them his home. Through the merger of Krishna's body, their soul has been released and they have attained salvation.*

Does that mean that hating God will ensure us of Moksh? The answer is 'No' because our stature is not equal to the stature of those who hated him. For us mortal beings attaching ourselves positively is the right way.

The attachment and bondage with the world take place due to ignorance of the mind and delusion. The attachment can be in very subtle forms, such as emotional bonding with wife, husband, children, grandchildren, and material things like house, car, property, and wealth.

A child can be attached to a doll for that matter and does not want to give it away. One can be attached to one's old, dilapidated car and does not want to give it away.

In the Bhagavad Gita, three types of attachment are highlighted: attachment to the results of actions (phala), attachment to actions themselves (karma), and attachment to one's own body and ego (deha and ahankara). These attachments bind individuals to the cycle of birth and death, preventing them from attaining liberation and ultimate union with the divine.

Illusion, or maya, is a concept intricately connected to attachment in the Bhagavad Gita. Maya refers to the deceptive nature of the material world, which makes us perceive things differently from their true essence. It creates a veil of ignorance, distorting our perception of reality and trapping us in the cycle of attachment and suffering.

The Bhagavad Gita teaches that the material world is temporary and constantly changing. It emphasizes that our true nature is eternal and beyond the physical realm. By identifying with the eternal soul rather than the temporary material body, we can break free from the illusion of attachment and experience lasting peace and joy.

Detachment is the antidote to attachment. It involves developing a sense of non-attachment towards the outcomes of our actions and cultivating an attitude of selflessness. Detachment does not mean indifference or apathy but rather a shift in perspective, recognizing that our identity lies beyond the temporary manifestations of the world.

To overcome attachment, the Bhagavad Gita provides practical guidance. It encourages individuals to perform their duties without attachment to the results, surrendering the fruits of their actions to the divine. Through selfless service, meditation, and cultivating devotion, one can gradually detach from the material world and find inner peace and spiritual fulfilment.

The Bhagavad Gita offers valuable lessons on attachment and illusion. It teaches us that true happiness and freedom lie in detaching ourselves from the temporary and transient aspects of life and connecting with our eternal nature.

Attachment can have a profound impact on our lives. When we become deeply attached to people, possessions, or outcomes, we often experience a rollercoaster of emotions. We may feel joy when our desires are fulfilled, but equally, we may experience disappointment, sorrow, and frustration when things don't go as planned. Attachment binds us to the fluctuations of the external world, leading to emotional instability and a constant longing for more.

It is what is happening to me. I am an emotional person, and my emotions make it difficult for me to work. At work, I first give leeway to colleagues and subordinates by sharing everything and later when they take advantage, I regret it. I don't maintain the distance required for each of these relations. In particular, I have been exploited by my subordinate. Through my reference he got the job and learned everything from me, I graded him fairly well then used me like a ladder to climb up. He has taken advantage of my freedom and has started to look for weaknesses in my work. I had no idea that people were so ungrateful, that they could use others for their own benefit. I have been connected to him from the very beginning, and so far, I have been detached. I've learned it the hard way, and I have come to understand the importance of being attached to a job rather than a person.

The Bhagavad Gita offers a path to liberation from the illusion of attachment. It teaches us to cultivate equanimity, to perform our duties without attachment to the results, and to surrender the outcomes to a higher power. By focusing on the present moment and recognizing the impermanence of material possessions and relationships, we can free ourselves from the chains of attachment and find inner peace.

Breaking the illusion of attachment requires self-awareness and introspection. We must examine our desires and attachments, questioning their true significance in our lives. Are these attachments bringing us lasting happiness, or are they simply feeding our ego and creating dependency? By recognizing the temporary nature of the material world, we can shift our focus towards the eternal and find fulfilment in spiritual growth rather than external acquisitions.

Let's understand through the story of Jadabharata from Bhagavat:

Many years ago, there used to live a king named Bharata. He was the son of Rishabha and used to live in a place known as Shalagrama. He thought of Vishnu all the time, even in his dreams and he had given up all thought of violence.

Once Bharata had gone to bathe in a river. A deer had also come to drink water there. While the deer was drinking water, there was the terrible roar of a lion. The deer gave a frightened leap and gave an untimely birth. The baby fell into the river. The mother deer died because of the leap. But Bharata rescued the baby deer from the water and brought it home to his ashrama (hermitage). Every day, the king fed the baby and slowly, the deer grew bigger. It wandered around the hermitage. Sometimes it even wandered out, but returned quickly as it was frightened of tigers. Asit grew older, the deer would leave the ashrama in the mornings and return in the evenings.

Bharata grew attached to the deer and forgot everything else. He had given up his kingdom, his sons, and his friends and forgotten them all. But he could not forget the deer. If the deer was late in returning to the ashrama, he would worry that it might have been eaten up by a wolf or a tiger or a lion. He would be happy only when the deer returned. And because Bharata thought about the deer so much, he forgot to think of Vishnu.

Many years passed. Bharata died watching the deer and thinking of it. Since he thought of the deer while dying, he was born as a deer in his next life. The only difference was that he was born as a jatismara deer, that is, a deer that remembered the incidents of its past life. As a deer, Bharata left his mother and came again to Shalagrama because he remembered his old place. He lived on dry leaves and dry grass and eventually died. He was reborn as a Jatismara brahmana.

In this life he was truly learned, well versed in all the shastras.

Since he had attained the supreme knowledge, he saw no point in reading the Vedas or in doing work. He kept to himself and spoke little, only when he had to. His body was dirty, his clothes were filthy, and he never cleaned his teeth. Because of this, people treated him badly. But since interaction with people was an obstacle to attaining supreme knowledge. Bharata kept up this pretence of beigh slightly mad. He moved so little that he came to known as Jababharata. He ate whatever was available to him. And when his father died, his brothers, nephews, and friends, gave him only dirty food to eat. Since he was strong and stout, they used him in their farming work.

The sage Kapila had an ashrama on the banks of the river Ikshumati. One day, the King of Soubira wanted to go there on a planaquin to learn words of wisdom from the sage. The servant of the king looked for palanquin-bearers who would carry the palanquin free of charge and found Bharata. So Bharata bore the palanquin along with the other bearers. But he walked slowly while the other bearers walked fast. The result was that the palanquin did not move smoothly. When scolded, the other bearers naturally blamed Bharata for this difficulty.

"What is wrong?" Asked the king of Bharata, "Haven't you borne the planquin only for a little while? How is it that you are tired? Can't you bear a little burden? You look quite strong to me."

Bharata's answer was this. "Who am I and who are you? What you have seen is only my body and your body. I am not my body and nor are your your body. Our atmans or souls are what we really are. My atman is not strong or tired, nor is it carrying your palanquin upon its shoulders."

Having said this, Bharata was quiet again. But the king got down from the palanquin and fell at his feet. He wanted to know who Bharata really was, for such words of wisdom do not come from an ordinary man. Bharata then told him the truth about the atman, which is never destroyed and takes up different bodies from one life to another. This is the jivatman. In additon, there is the paramatman, which is Vishnu and is everywhere. There is no difference between the jivatman and the parmatman and the person who has realized this is truly wise. To think that the jivatman is different from the parmatman is to suffer from maya or illusion.

Moral of the story: The moral of the story is that we should not become attached to things which are bound to have negative impact in our lives. Breaking the illusion of attachment requires self-awareness and introspection. We must examine our desires and attachments, questioning their true significance in our lives. Are these attachments bringing us lasting happiness, or are they simply feeding our ego and creating dependency? By recognizing the temporary nature of the material world, we can shift our focus towards the eternal and find fulfilment in spiritual growth rather than external acquisitions.

Cultivating detachment is a gradual process that requires practice and discipline. It involves developing an attitude of non-possessiveness, letting go of the need to control outcomes, and accepting the impermanence of life. By embracing detachment, we open ourselves up to the beauty of the present moment and release the burden of expectations.

True freedom is found in detaching ourselves from the illusion of attachment. It is the freedom to be unaffected by external circumstances, to experience joy and peace regardless of the outcomes. By transcending attachment, we connect with our inner essence, the eternal soul that is beyond the fluctuations of the material world.

Attachment is indeed an illusion, as the Bhagavad Gita teaches us. By recognizing the transient nature of the material world and cultivating detachment, we can break free from the chains of attachment and experience true freedom and spiritual enlightenment.

Letting go of all your attachments will bring you so much peace. You can't even imagine how blissful you will feel the moment you decide to let go of your need to control everything, to let go of your need to have and possess everything, acting like nothing will ever come to an end. It all does. You don't want to accept this fact now, but you will, one day, you have no choice.

My Guru taught me to be attached to your true cause. What is your true cause?

The true cause is to be attached to yourself, your good deeds, your karma.

By implanting an embryo inside the womb of a woman, God bring new life to us. He is the one who is giving our soul a body to live in. He supports us through parents when we can't take care of ourselves. He is making it possible for us to buy a home in this material world from the space he owns. He will give us the capacity to make a living and provide resources that belong to him for our lives. We are going to use all the stuff he owns, and we need to keep everything in this world when our end is here. In the end we are taking nothing with us. And yet we continue to hoard material stuff and make ourselves dependent on it. We'll no longer be concerned about attachment to people or material things when we realize the eternal truth that we are a soul. The soul is neither born, nor does it ever die; nor having once existed, does it ever cease to be. The soul is devoid of birth, eternal, immortal and ageless. When the body is destroyed, it won't be destroyed.

You are attached to people because you fear they are going to leave you, you fear that they are going to get sick and die one day and you will be left all alone; you are attached to your job because you fear that if you lose it, you will no longer have money to support yourself and your family, etc. There is nothing wrong in wanting to have your family healthy and alive; there is nothing wrong in wanting to keep your job to support your family, but you need to accept this idea that it can all come to an end at any time. This is the difference between love and attachment. Love your friends, love your family, love your job, your house, your life, but don't get attached to any of them, because they are not going to be present in your life forever. You are not going to be on this planet forever.

If you know that you are going to leave everything here, you will remain attached to your true cause.

Let us embark on this transformative journey, embracing the wisdom of the Bhagavad Gita and finding lasting peace and fulfilment within ourselves. Let us be attached to our true cause.

"Go on efficiently doing your duty at all times without attachment. Doing work without the attachment, man attains the Supreme." – Bhagvad Gita

In the next chapter, we will find out about jealousy which comes from greed.

6

Jealousy

- You don't trust your partner when you're not together.
- You get concerned when they mention other people.
- You constantly check their social media to see what they're doing.
- You think they're cheating on you.
- You're attempting to control your partner's behaviour.
- You're feeling bad seeing them buying a new car.
- You're feeling bad seeing them happy.

Just about each one of us feels jealous or envious occasionally. However, when these emotions start to become overwhelming, it can trigger concerns about inadequacy or feeling of ill will towards others. It can also bring about symptoms of stress. In some cases, it can lead to depression. It is a major cause of depression among people. While loneliness is one of the main causes of depression, jealousy is the second biggest reason leading to many associated illnesses.

Jealousy is quite prevalent in our lives. People are jealous of everyone & everything around them. It is manifested in different ways. Sometimes through actions, sometimes through words, sometimes through anger, body gestures, and other forms of expressions. But when we are confronted, we obviously refuse being jealous because we live in denial. We live in a dual state of mind. Our words say something, and our actions indicate otherwise. We live in complete contradiction of our real self. We all feel and observe jealousy being demonstrated in different ways. Whether it is the professional arena, family life or friends circle jealousy is invariably and inevitably seen & felt everywhere.

Professionally, we demean people, pull them down, create obstacles & adverse situations, backstab them, speak ill about them, and criticize them. Often exploiting situations and circumstances to work to our advantage. A colleague working in a different department is jealous of other colleague regardless of his work profile & level in the organisation without any connection with him due to jealousy. A colleague in the same department is jealous because the other colleague has been promoted and she is not. A superior to whom a subordinate once reported is jealous because she doesn't want to see her growing under someone else's watch and trying to create all kinds of hurdles stooping to lowest levels of jealousy. Someone's jealous of another for the personality traits they have, like communication skills, walking ability, talking, and dressing abilities, different relationships, skill sets, physical assets, and that sort of thing. A line manager is jealous of his direct subordinate being smarter than him and don't want to see him growing due to his own insecurity that one day the subordinate may surpass him. Similarly, a subordinate is jealous of his superior's standing in the company and his closeness to another subordinate. Jealousy knows no boundaries. One could have the most trivial of the reasons to be jealous. It stems from inner insecurities and fears.

A brother in a family is jealous of how his brother has become successful, the group of friends he surrounds himself with, his sense of style, his ability to talk, his social standing, house, car, wife, job, and many other reasons. Similarly, for the same reasons, a sister is jealous of another sister. We have always sworn by a bond between a sister and a brother but, even a sister is jealous of her brother. She doesn't have her beloved brother doing as well as her other brother. Her sister-in-law is not behaving as per her expected norms of behaviour. She is being swallowed up by her ego and she will go to any length in order to destroy the family bond. For her beauty, closeness to family members, education, career, and smallest of attributes, a daughter in law is jealous of another daughter in law. Jealousy's not over at the siblings. It's a lot farther than the siblings. His son is jealous of the fact that his father has been more revered in society, and so on. The thing with jealousy is that it works in mysterious ways. You can expect it from the most unexpected person in the most whimsical way.

Jealousy has the power to destroy relationships, friendships, family bonds, careers, reputations, and one's stature in the society. We all have witnessed such situations and people in our lives.

It's the same thing that happened in my friend's family. His brother's wife had destroyed the family bond with her jealousy of his wife. She was jealous of her sister in law's beauty, work, ethics, family background, popularity & respect within the family. She has changed the dynamics of this house through her husband instead of keeping the family together. She has damaged her reputation in a slow and gradual way through bad planning and actions. She was playing with every member of the family, changing everything. The brothers hate each other, the daughter in law hates each other and every member of the family can't stand another member of the family. A once stronger bond is no longer intact. Obviously, that's what happened when his parents were not there. The fundamental link that held the whole family together was his parents.

Let us understand why human beings are jealous of other human beings. Why are we so focused on proving ourselves right and all others wrong. Constantly being captious of everyone, always judging every action only leads to negativity. Remember every small thought when multiplied has a compounding effect. A small negative thought compounds and turns our personality into a pessimistic person and eventually abhorrent.

What is jealousy?

Jealousy is holding onto something you already have. You might experience jealousy in a relationship when you perceive a threat or worry that the relationship is changing in a negative way. Jealousy is comparison and we have been taught to compare; we have been conditioned to compare since our childhood days. We have often been compared for our education, physical appearance, our financial status, our success and numerous other aspects and that small comparison which looked insignificant at a point in our life has taken a bigger form which is consciously or subconsciously reflected in our behaviour. Somebody else has a better house, somebody else has a more beautiful body, somebody else has more money, somebody else has a more charismatic personality.

Compare, go on comparing yourself with everybody else you pass by, and great jealousy will be the outcome; it is the by-product of the conditioning for comparison.

Ask yourself:

- Am I jealous of others?
- If yes, why am I jealous of others?
- How do I feel when I am jealous?

When you find the answers, you will notice that intentionally or unintentionally you are jealous of others. It reflects in your thoughts, gestures, words, and actions. You will notice that it's not a pleasant feeling. It is shaping your personality in a negative way.

This is exactly how I used to feel early in my professional life. I used to be jealous of my colleague's success because we had the same qualification & experience, and I was better in academics then he was. I felt bad when he was promoted and I was not, when he was appreciated, and I was not. I'd say bad things about him to my colleagues and expect sympathy from them, I'd have a bad mood at home and spoil my personal time with my wife who'd been brooding on the same subject. I realized later that the same crew had been enjoying my misery and were making fun of me behind my back. Eventually, I realized that talking to them about my feelings was useless, and with experience, I realized that it was useless to feel jealous. There's a life path for both of us, and it should have been different. I've learned to look back on my life journey and judge its success or failure from that point of view.

Why is it that we are so focused on what other people have accomplished in their lives? What type of clothes are they wearing, what are they eating, what are they drinking, where are they living, which car they are driving, which destination they are traveling, who are they talking, what they are talking about and so on. There are ups and downs in everyone's life. On our side, grass is always greener and grayer on the other side.

If we drop comparing, jealousy disappears. Then we simply know we are we, and we are nobody else, and there is no need. It is good that we don't compare ourselves with trees, otherwise we will start feeling very jealous: why are we not green? And why has existence been so hard on us - and no flowers? It is better that we don't compare with birds, with rivers, with mountains; otherwise, we will suffer. We only compare with human beings, because we have been conditioned to compare only with human beings; we don't compare with peacocks and with parrots. Otherwise, our jealousy would be more and more: we would be so burdened by jealousy that we would not be able to live at all.

Comparison is a very foolish attitude, because each person is unique and incomparable. Once this understanding settles in you, jealousy disappears. Each is unique and incomparable. You are just yourself: nobody has ever been like you, and nobody will ever be like you. And you need not be like anybody else, either. Existence creates only originals; it does not believe in carbon copies.

Next door great things are happening: the grass is greener; the roses are rosier. Everybody seems to be so happy - except yourself. You are continuously comparing. And the same is the case with the others, they are comparing too. Maybe they think the grass in your lawn is greener - it always looks greener from the distance - that you have a more beautiful wife.... You are tired, you cannot believe why you allowed yourself to be trapped by this woman, you don't know how to get rid of her – and the neighbour may be jealous of you, that you have such a beautiful wife! And you may be jealous of him....

Everybody is jealous of everybody else. And out of jealousy we create such hell, and out of jealousy we become very mean. If everybody is in misery, it feels good; if everybody is losing, it feels good. If everybody is happy and succeeding, it tastes very bitter.

But why does the idea of the other enter in your head in the first place? Again, let me remind you:

Because you have not allowed your own juices to flow; you have not allowed your own blissfulness to grow, you have not allowed your own being to bloom. Hence you feel empty inside, and you look at each and everybody's outside because only the outside can be seen.
You know your inside, and you know the others' outside: that creates jealousy.

They know your outside, and they know their inside: that creates jealousy. Nobody else knows your inside. There you know you are nothing, worthless. And the others on the outside look so smiling. Their smiles may be phony, but how can you know that they are phony? Maybe their hearts are also smiling. You know your smile is phony, because your heart is not smiling at all, it may be crying and weeping.

You know your interiority, and only you know it, nobody else. And you know everybody's exterior, and their exterior people have made it beautiful. Exteriors are showpieces and they are very deceptive.

Let us understand jealousy through an ancient Sufi story:

A man was very much burdened by his suffering. He used to pray every day to God, "Why me? Everybody seems to be so happy, why am only I in such suffering?" One day, out of great desperation, he prayed to God, "You can give me anybody else's suffering and I am ready to accept it. But take mine, I cannot bear it anymore."

That night he had a beautiful dream very beautiful and very revealing. He had a dream that night that God appeared in the sky, and he said to everybody, "Bring all your sufferings into the temple." Everybody was tired of his suffering - in fact everybody has prayed some time or other, "I am ready to accept anybody else's suffering, but take mine away; this is too much, it is unbearable."
So everybody gathered his own sufferings into bags, and they reached the temple, and they were looking very happy; the day has come, their prayer has been heard. And this man also rushed to the temple.
And then God said, "Put your bags by the walls." All the bags were put by the walls, and then God declared: "Now you can choose. Anybody can take any bag."
And the most surprising thing was this: that this man who had been praying always, rushed towards his bag before anybody else could choose it! But he was in for a surprise because everybody rushed to his own bag, and everybody was happy to choose it again. What was the matter? For the first time, everybody had seen others' miseries, others' sufferings - their bags were as big, or even bigger!
And the second problem was, one had become accustomed to one's own

sufferings. Now to choose somebody else's - who knows what kind of sufferings will be inside the bag? Why bother? At least you are familiar with your own sufferings, and you have become accustomed to them, and they are tolerable. For so many years you have tolerated them - why choose the unknown?

And everybody went home happy. Nothing had changed, they were bringing the same suffering back, but everybody was happy and smiling and joyous that he could get his own bag back.

In the morning he prayed to God, and he said, "Thank you for the dream; I will never ask again. Whatsoever you have given me is good for me, it must be good for me; that's why you have given it to me."

Because of jealousy you are in constant suffering; you become mean to others. And because of jealousy you start becoming fake because you start pretending. You start pretending things that you don't have, you start pretending things which you can't have, which are not natural to you. You become more and more artificial. Imitating others, competing with others, what else can you do? If somebody has something and you don't have it, and you don't have a natural possibility of having it, the only way is to have some cheap substitute for it.

The jealous man lives in hell. Drop comparing and jealousy disappears, meanness disappears, phoniness disappears. But you can drop it only if you start growing your inner treasures; there is no other way.

Krishna says grow up, become a more and more authentic individual. Love yourself and respect yourself the way existence has made you, and then immediately the doors of heaven open for you. They were always open; you had simply not looked at them.

How can we avoid jealousy?

I stated above that I was jealous of my colleague, and it hurt me a lot. How did I overcome it?

I ceased comparing myself to others. Instead, I've shifted to comparing my present self with my past—where I stood just a few years ago, where I stand now, and what I aim to accomplish in the future. Additionally, I came to the realization that my comparisons were limited to the positive aspects of someone's life, neglecting their struggles. For a fair comparison, it's crucial to consider both sides accurately. We're all fortunate to be where we are. This change in perspective has significantly aided my healing process. I've been decluttering unnecessary thoughts from my mind, lightening the mental load. As a result, I feel more at ease and unburdened.

Here are a few steps that I think we can follow to avoid jealousy:

Trace it back to its source: Examining your jealous feelings can give you insight on where it come from:
- Your sister's new relationship causes jealousy because you haven't had much luck dating and worry, you'll never find the right person.
- Your coworker's promotion makes you feel jealous because you believe you aren't good enough at your job to get a promotion yourself.
- When your partner starts spending a lot of time with a new friend, you feel jealous because that was the first sign you noticed when a previous partner cheated.

Whether your jealousy stems from insecurity, fear, or past relationship patterns, knowing more about the causes can help you figure out how to confront it.
Maybe you have an open conversation with your supervisor about getting on track for promotion, resolve to try a different approach to dating, or talk to your partner about your feelings.

Voice your concerns: If your partner's actions (or someone else's actions toward your partner) trigger jealous feelings, bring this up with your partner as soon as possible.
Your partner may not have noticed the behaviour, or they may not have realized how you felt about it. Use the opportunity to talk over any relationship boundaries you might want to revisit or discuss ways to keep your relationship strong.
If you trust your partner but have doubts because of past relationship experiences, try finding a few ways you both can help improve the situation.
If you feel nervous about mentioning jealous feelings, try to remember they're totally normal. Your partner might even have had some jealous feelings of their own at some point.

Talk to a trusted friend: Jealousy can sometimes give you a slightly warped sense of reality. You might wonder if that nonverbal flirting you swear you saw happened.

Sometimes, voicing these concerns to a third party can make the situation less frightening and help you gain some perspective.

Put a different spin on jealousy: Jealousy can be a complex, strong emotion, and you might not feel very good when you're dealing with it. But instead of thinking of it as something negative, try looking at it as a helpful source of information.

Consider the full picture: Jealousy sometimes develops in response to a partial picture. In other words, you might be comparing yourself and your own achievements and attributes to an idealized or incomplete view of someone else.

But you never truly know what someone's going through, especially when you're just looking at social media. Your college friend with the Facebook photos of her and her husband out in a meadow, looking so carefree and happy? For all you know, they argued all the way out there and they're sweating bullets under all that matching plaid.

Practice gratitude for what you have: A little gratitude can go a long way. It can not only reduce feelings of jealousy, but also relieve stress. You might not have everything you want. Most of us don't. But you probably have at least some of what you want. Maybe you even have some good things in your life you didn't expect. This can help whether you're eyeing your friend's fancy new bike or wishing your partner didn't spend quite so much time with friends.

Remind yourself of your sturdy, reliable bike that gets you where you need to go. Consider the benefits of having a partner who appreciates the value of friendship. Even appreciating positive things in your life that don't relate to jealousy can help you realize that, while your life may not be perfect (but whose life is?), you've still got some good things going for you.

Practice in-the-moment coping techniques: Coping with jealousy as it comes up won't help you work through underlying causes. But it can help to keep the distress at bay until you can deal with the underlying issues. Explore underlying issues. Jealousy that persists and causes distress can sometimes relate to or self-anxiety esteem issues, explains. "Learning how to deal with either issue can automatically help soothe jealousy." One way to approach low self-esteem involves identifying personal values, such as compassion, communication, or honesty. This helps because it lets you check whether you're upholding these values in your daily life.

It also gives you a chance to notice your positive traits and review what's important to you. This can increase your sense of self-respect and may help decrease distressing feelings of inferiority or competitiveness.

Anxiety can have a range of symptoms that might be more difficult to address on your own. Coping techniques can help, but therapy can also be a good option.

- Increase acceptance around anxious feelings so they don't overwhelm you.
- Recognize unwanted or distressing thoughts so you can challenge and replace them.

Remember your own value: When jealousy prompts you to compare yourself to others, your self-worth can end up taking a hit. Your life might be enviable to someone else, after all. But jealousy can make you feel like nothing you have is good enough. Research exploring a possible link between jealousy and self-esteem found evidence to suggest jealousy can develop when you face a threat to your self-esteem.

To combat low self-esteem:

- Remind yourself of things you do well.
- Practice self-compassion (in other words, treat yourself the way you would a close friend).
- Practice daily affirmations or exchange them with your partner.
- Remind yourself of the things you value in your partner and relationship.

- Make time to do things you enjoy.

Practice mindfulness: Mindfulness techniques help you pay attention to your thoughts and feelings as they come up without judging or criticizing them. Increasing your awareness around jealousy can help you notice any patterns it follows, including things that happen before you feel jealous.

Mindfulness can also help you feel more comfortable with jealousy. For example, it can help you notice and accept your jealous feelings for what they are — part of your emotional experience — and move on.

Not judging the jealousy, or yourself for feeling it, can help keep it from affecting you negatively.

Give it time: If you've experienced jealousy before, you probably already know that jealousy fades with time. It might feel less intense after you deal with your feelings, of course, but it can also lessen once whatever you felt jealous about is over.

According to research that looked at the experience of jealousy, people are generally more likely to feel jealous right before something happens, rather than after.

As time passes, you're also less likely to feel the need to compare yourself or your circumstances to someone else. But the positive feelings you have stay.

So, while you might feel jealous as your best friend's wedding date approaches, on the day after the wedding you might feel less jealous and more just happy for your friend.

Talk to a therapist: If you're having trouble coping with jealous thoughts on your own, talking to a therapist can help.

It's not always easy to talk about jealousy. You might feel even more uncomfortable sharing these thoughts with someone you don't know. But a good therapist will meet you with kindness and compassion.

Plus, they know better than anyone that jealousy is a normal emotion that everyone feels at some point.

Here are a few signs that suggest talking to a therapist could be helpful:

- Jealousy leads to obsessive or fixated thoughts.
- You notice compulsive behaviours.
- Jealous thoughts become uncontrollable or intrusive.
- You have violent thoughts or urges.
- Jealous feelings trigger problematic behaviours, like following your partner or checking up on them constantly.
- Jealousy affects your day-to-day life, prevents you from doing things you want to do, or causes other distress.

"If you constantly need to check out your social media feed, your partner's phone, or what the people in line at Starbucks are wearing, then you can no longer be present in your own life, and that's a problem,".

Jealousy can help you focus on who (and what) you care about. It doesn't have to cause problems for you or your relationships. It can even help relationships become stronger in some cases. It all comes down to how you use it.

As per my Guru, material jealousy pulls down our consciousness. But if jealousy is spiritualized, it becomes constructive and inspires us to move ahead. How can jealousy be spiritualized? By simply replacing material jealousy with spiritual feelings.

Asking ourselves questions like how our friend has achieved closeness to God and we have not?

When it comes to comparing material possessions, it's important to look at those less fortunate than us and express gratitude to the higher power for blessing us with more than what countless others lack. Equally, it's beneficial to observe those who have achieved significant spiritual growth. Doing so can inspire us to aspire to greater heights in our own spiritual journey.

Today, let's bring a small change in our lives. Let us no longer feel insecure & jealous. Let us focus on our life. Let us build positive thoughts.

Let us be indifferent towards everyone and focus on our life.

In the next chapter we will talk about Pride and how it makes the mighty fall.

7
Pride

- You try to avoid feelings of guilt and shame.
- You struggle to trust or listen to your leaders.
- You become jealous if someone is better than you.
- If you do not fix a situation, you feel that no one else will.
- You tend to point out the mistakes of others when you are annoyed.
- You believe that if people do not take your advice, they will regret it later.
- You are concerned that people will notice your flaws and form negative opinions of you.
- You often pretend that you are doing well, even when you are struggling internally.
- You believe that if there was something wrong with you, you would be the first to know.
- You tend to manipulate situations to make others appear guilty or at fault (blame-shfting).
- When you disagree with someone, you tend to think that they are overly emotional or flawed.
- You tend to say or do things to ensure that people think highly of you (people-pleasing).
- You believe that you deserve a better life, blessings, and good things because you do the right things and work hard (entitlement).

After reflecting, I've come to realize that some of these tendencies are consciously or subconsciously carried over into my own behavior. I've been trying to avoid the feeling of guilt and shame. I've had a hard time trusting my leaders. I've been relying too much on myself, and I've always felt that only I can solve my problems, not believe in the process, not believe in God. For every problem, I used to have a habit of putting my mistakes on others. I could feel a sense of entitlement. This is something that we all think all the time.

Ask yourself:

- Do I exhibit such behavior?
- If yes, why do I exhibit such behavior?

When I was a kid, I was inhibited and diffident. That's because I was an introverted person. I was hesitant to initiate a discussion. People perceived that I am an arrogant person. It worked against me all the time. Everyone thought I was not interested in talking. While the reality was different, I paid the price for it because people responded in the same way. It affects me till date. In today's world of intolerance people try to pull me down through their actions. Although, I mean no hard feelings towards anyone, I was displaying a behavior of pride.

Pride is often rooted in deep insecurity, fear, and feelings of unworthiness. Prideful individuals may often feel small, overlooked, insecure, powerless, and unloved. To conceal these feelings from the world, they put on a false mask of perfection, confidence, and engage in attention-seeking behaviours.

What is the definition of Pride?

The definition of pride refers to "an unreasonable sense of superiority in one's talents, beauty, wealth, social rank, and other such factors; feeling no need for God and relying entirely on oneself; looking down on others; feeling entitled to certain things due to hard work; exhibiting disdainful behaviour, insolence, or arrogance."

Characteristics of Egoïstic people are:

- They've overconfidence.
- It's difficult to handle them.
- They can insult anyone easily.
- They're self-obsessed.

- They lack empathy.

Pride itself is not a problem—excessive pride is.

Arrogant people tend to score high on narcissism. Excessive pride diminishes self-awareness Like an arrogant leader who's always exaggerating his achievements to denigrate his rivals.

My ex-boss displayed narcissistic behaviour in the office. He'd been exaggerating his minor accomplishments and belittling other people's great achievements. It was as if he were the only one who knew everything. In his department and many others, he had often reproached colleagues who worked in office with impunity. He wielded power by controlling people under him through unreasonable behaviour and preposterous issues. He'd interfered with the works of others, picked up errors along the way in order to convince everyone else and himself that he was correct. He was hated by everyone, but people who worked under him couldn't afford to go against him. He'd been an extremely self centered and selfish man.

"*Self-centered people have only one topic to talk about...THEMSELVES.*"— **Stef Harder**

Ask yourself:

- Do I exhibit arrogant behaviour?
- Do I hurt people in doing so?

Excessive ego fosters a false belief of being superior, leading individuals to think they are the best. This creates an artificial sense of superiority over others. Individuals driven by such ego rarely engage in direct confrontation. Instead, they resort to manipulation and unfair tactics to control and influence others. Their leadership style stems from insecurity since they are unable to exert control through logic. Consequently, they resort to dominating through instilling fear.

Excessive pride is an exaggerated appreciation of oneself by devaluating others—we turn other people into our competitors.

"I know" is youngsters' response by default. They are not wired to listen. Adolescents believe they have all the answers. That's not an issue unless they carry that arrogant behaviour into adulthood.

In my personal circle, I have seen kids of friends exhibiting pompous behaviour. Their behaviour reflects arrogance emanating from their parents' status in the society. One of the kid's natural responses to any question is 'I know it' even before the question is asked. Another kid flaunts his fathers' financial status, car, and other material possessions all the time and keeps saying: we have the biggest car, I have so many girlfriends. Imagine if this is the condition of their behaviour now what will happen when they grow up regardless of what they become. They would still treat people with indignation.

Excessive pride makes us ignorant. It harms our relationships too—nobody likes being with a know-it-all. While pride can undoubtedly lead to arrogant displays, it can also motivate us to give our best. Pride is like a condiment—it adds flavour to your life. A little touch can make it more pleasurable or exciting. In excess, it makes everything unpleasant.

Feeling proud is not the same as being proud. Acknowledging your strengths and achievements reinforces positive behaviour. It inspires you to give more. However, being proud is living under a distorted notion. We exaggerate our perception of self to feel superior.

Pride is rooted in the same principle as envy—we define our self-worth by comparing to others. But, unlike envy, rather than wanting what others have, we need to disparage them to feel superior. Buddhism recognizes six poisons that harm our perception and behaviour. Pride is the most pervasive. Pride is a poison because it's the basis for disrespecting others and for creating suffering in our lives.

Excessive pride is an exaggerated appreciation of oneself by devaluating others. It is often driven by poor self-worth. We are so insecure that we compensate by feeling superior. And look for others' flaws as a way to disguise our own.

We spend too much time competing with other people. They taught us that winners take all. Most people believe that being successful requires humiliating or defeating others.

As Thubten Chodron said, "Why do we have to put someone down to feel good?"

Buddhists encourage confidence and honesty with oneself. Pride is demeaning other people or feeling an aversion to others. Instead of nurturing self-growth, we compete and want to defeat others.

Excessive pride prevents the growth of other virtues. It becomes too uncomfortable to recognize our shortcoming or mistakes. Pride makes us believe we are always right.

How can we become more compassionate if we are already so great?

Pride has many flavours—actually seven, according to **Thubten Chodron.** The Seven Flavors of Pride

In one of her teachings, the American Buddhist explains the different flavours that pride takes. Each has self-indulgent nuances. But they all leave a bitter aftertaste.

1. Pride over the inferior: The first type of pride is the most common. We compare ourselves to others in terms of education, social standing, health, beauty, physical attributes, or other aspects.

This happens when we, in fact, are better than somebody else in one of those aspects. We compare our strengths to someone else's weakness. And look down on them.

2. Great Pride: This happens when we can't accept that we are equal to others in a particular aspect. Our competitive mode doesn't leave us in peace. We see others as competitors that we must defeat.

Great pride is a culture view. That's what kids learn from their parents. They associate getting recognition to beating someone else.

Even when we go for a run or bike ride, we need stats to prove that we are better. All we care is bragging about our superior performance, not the joy of exercising.

As Chodron explains, parents don't ask their children if they had fun during a match. But praise their kids when they beat others. Children learn that recognition matters more than having joy.

Great pride is the enemy of collaboration—instead of thinking of the group welfare, we want to win.

3. Pride of Pride: This is when we compare ourselves to others—in any aspect—and are actually inferior.

Instead of accepting the fact, we look for something that will make us proud. For example, you might say, "I might not be as good taking pictures as X, but I'm a more honest person."

You focus on another quality that will help overcome your weakness. One that will make you feel morally superior. You defeat the other person by attacking their virtues.

It can be something insignificant, but still, you find a way to discredit your 'opponents' by finding their moral flaw.

4. Pride of the sense of "I": This is thinking of yourself as being perfect.

You turn one experience into something that makes you feel the king of the world. Like when you break a rule or do something that makes you feel unique.

5. Evident or manifest pride: This is where we are proud about the qualities or abilities that we don't have. But we think we do.

You see it all the time—people get attached to an illusion. They think they are proficient at something but are clueless.

Manifest pride is when we believe we are better, wiser, more spiritual, or virtuous than we are.

6. Feeling slightly less pride: This is when we feel proud of our weaknesses. It's the case of those who play the victim role because it gives them power—others pay attention.

We make ourselves insignificant by putting ourselves down. We make a big deal of small flaws to feel at the centre of the world.

The need to compete with others makes us cling to an exaggerated image of ourselves—in this case, a negative one. We become proud of being a victim.

7. Distorted pride: The last type of pride is about bragging about our non-virtues.

It's the feeling of superiority when someone cheats and doesn't get caught. Think of those who lie in the tax declaration or frame someone else at work for a mistake they did.

Distorted pride is when our morality is full of holes, but we feel superior because we got away with it.

The Antidote to Excessive Pride

Unfortunately, there's no simple cure. We spend our entire lives feeding our ego—it takes time to reframe that relationship.

Start by reflecting on the role pride plays in your life.

Acknowledge the difference between feeling proud and being proud. The first is the joy of a job well done. The latter is an exaggerated, distorted version of who you are.

You can turn your pride into a means for development. Inquire your pride and see how it manifests. Excessive pride signals what we must further develop.

Ask yourself:

- Do I feel insecure about a particular aspect of myself?
- Do I have a distorted perception of my strengths or abilities?
- Do I see others as rivals or collaborators?

As Sophocles said, "All men make mistakes, but a good man yields when he knows his course is wrong and repairs the evil. The only crime is pride."

Buddhism teaches to overcome excessive pride by cultivating equanimity and love for others. An appreciation for life and people removes the need to defeat them—there's no need to compete.

Reconnecting ourselves with what we don't know keeps our ego in check.

Intellect humility can help overcome our pride too. Do you think you know a lot about a particular topic? Focus on something complicated that you don't master. Surround yourself with people who know more than you do.

Pride is being attached to an exaggerated image of our self—we must let go of that dependence.

Thubten Chodron recommends contemplating that everything we have come from others.

Reflect that everything you do, know, are or have it's not yours to start with. Everything happened due to the efforts and kindness of somebody else.

- Do you feel proud of your body? Your parents gave it to you.
- Are you proud of your car? Reflect on everybody involved in designing, building, and distributing the vehicle. Somebody else created it—not you.
- Do you feel proud of your appearance? There are so many better-looking people than you.

Trace the origin of whatever you feel proud—consider everyone who participated in the process.

Your knowledge is not yours alone. Your parents, teachers, professors, coaches, and many more contributed to your learning experience.

The world is an interconnected whole—no person or nation can be truly isolated. Reflecting on that will keep your pride under control. Everything we own or achieve is a consequence of collaboration with others.

Pride poisons our life. It creates an inflated version of self that we must defend at all costs. We take everything as criticism—we are under attack.

Don't turn life into an unpleasant experience. Work on deflating your ego. When your identity no longer is at stake, you won't need to fight with others.

Recover the pleasure of playing—life is not a match to be won but enjoyed. Acknowledge the good, avoid the pressure to defeat others.

You wouldn't accomplish anything without the help of other people. Pride has no room when we understand it's better to be surrounded by collaborators rather than competitors.

The signs of Pride are as below:

EGO SELF	HIGER SELF
Lives in victim mentality	Takes accountability to create a different reality
Scarcity mindset	Abundance mindset
Sees mistakes	Sees lessons
Complains about everything	Grateful and find joy in the little moment

Three Prongs of False Ego

Our false ego often acts like a trident that pierces us with three prongs: grandiosity, blame, and shame.

Grandiosity: When we set out to achieve something, our false ego makes us believe we are extraordinary and entitled to blaze our way to success. Such grandiosity often makes us look down on others who we think are not as talented as we are. By such condescension, the false ego makes us difficult for others to live with. And by distancing us from others, it makes us lonely and unhappy even when our grandiose dreams come true.

Blame: When we can't actualize our grandiose dreams, the false ego tries to protect itself by blaming others. When we keep looking for scapegoats and refuse to take responsibility for our shortcomings and mistakes, we can't grow; instead, we stagnate or even degrade, thereby setting ourselves up for misery.

Shame: When the false ego can't find anyone to blame, it starts imploding. It beats us down, making us believe we are worthless, useless, and hopeless. By pitting us against ourselves, shame strips us of our energy for self-improvement and makes us depressed or even suicidal.

There are 3 stories from Bhagavata that shows manifestation of False Ego in good and bad ways:

The Story of Bali Maharaj and Vamanadeva:

Srimad-Bhagavatam relates how Bali Maharaja and his soldiers once ousted Indra from his rule of the heavenly planets. When Lord Vishnu, disguised as Vamanadeva, a brahmana boy, appeared before Bali Maharaja to recover Indra's opulence, He asked for three paces of land according to the measurement of His steps. The charitably minded Bali Maharaja offered to give Him anything – even a planet of his own – but Vamanadeva declined the offer, saying He wanted only what He could cover in three steps. Ultimately, in just two steps the Lord took away everything from Bali Maharaja, who then surrendered himself at the lotus feet of the Lord and asked Him to place the third step on his head. For this deed, Bali is famed as the exemplar of full surrender unto the Lord.

Bali Maharaja had a little trace of false ego connected with his position as the emperor of all the worlds. While offering three steps of land to the Lord, **Bali was proud that he could offer so much more.** But his pride was not the same as the pride of defiance that constitutes the conditioned soul's resistance against the authority of the Lord. Bali is a mahajana, one of the leading spiritual authorities glorified in the Srimad-Bhagavatam, and he demonstrated surrender to the Lord. If his false ego had been a significant obstacle, then he would have resisted surrender, or in other words, pride would have interfered with his surrender. So, any little pride or apparent false ego found in Bali was an insignificant remnant of the influence of the material modes of nature, and by the mercy of Krishna as Vamanadeva, that little trace was cleansed away.

The story of Sudama Vipra and Krishna:

The story of Sudama Vipra, told in chapters eighty and eighty-one of the Tenth Canto of Srimad-Bhagavatam, is another beautiful narration. Sudama was a poverty-stricken brahmana (vipra), and though he had nothing, he was quite content, being free of material desires. At the request of his wife, who desired some relief from their poverty, he visited the Lord in His palace in Dwarka. Before he left home, his wife begged some simple chipped rice from neighbors to offer the Lord as a gift. When Sudama hesitated to offer the paltry rice to the Lord, He grabbed it anyway and ate a fistful of it. When He was about to have a second fistful, His wife Rukmini Devi stopped Him because (unbeknown to Sudama) she had already awarded Sudama immense wealth at his home and had nothing more to give except herself.

The Lord generally does not bestow material blessings upon His devotees, because they may be entrapped again in the material world, characterized by continuous birth, death, old age, and disease, yet He gave immense wealth to Sudama. In his commentary on this episode, Sri Jiva Goswami mentions that **Sudama's last trace of illusion lay in the subtle pride of being a renounced brahmana**. This trace was destroyed by his contemplating the Supreme Lord's submission to His devotees. The Lord's bestowing wealth on Sudama was the Lord's way of reciprocating Sudama's love. Krishna thought, "I cannot repay Sudama's exclusive love for Me, but let Me give him some material opulence."

Krishna acts in a very personal way with those He favors, and not everyone's spiritual needs are the same. If He takes away a particular person's wealth, the goal is not simply to take away the wealth, but to enrich that person in spiritual understanding. Others may not need it. For example, His pure devotees are not attached to wealth. For them, whether they have it or not is irrelevant. Some of them have wealth, while others don't. Krishna's special mercy and His giving of wealth do not necessarily go together, as the way His special mercy manifests depends on the particular devotee. Both giving and taking away can be His mercy.

The story of Indra and Krishna: False Ego Returns:

Indra, the king of heavenly planets, is a devotee of the Lord, though not a completely pure devotee. He knows that Krishna is supreme, but due to false ego he is possessive of his rule of the celestial kingdom. This impurity was on display during the govardhana-lila (Bhagavatam 10.25), when he became furious because the Vrajavasis, the residents of Vrindavan, accepted Krishna as their Lord and offered Him a sacrifice originally intended for Indra. The punishment Indra inflicted on the Vrajavasis was way beyond reasonable for the supposed offense the Vrajavasis had committed. For example, if we do not pay our utility bill, the city just disconnects the supply and does not punish us. Indra could have done something like that rather than attacking the Vrajavasis with a storm meant to destroy Vrindavan and every living thing in it. Indra's action shows the pitfall of material opulence for one who is not completely pure.

Attachment, pride, and anger all arise from material lust, which at its root is the desire to be the Lord. Indra exhibited this in its fullest sense because he holds the exalted position of lord of the heavens. Instead of representing Krishna, the ultimate Lord, as his agent, Indra became independent-minded and wanted to enjoy in opposition to Krishna. When this kind of attachment happens, one becomes angry and bewildered, and finally with lost intelligence one performs a destructive act. Indra was especially angry because he saw that the Vrajavasis canceled his puja not simply because of laziness or some small material pride but because they accepted Krishna as the Lord of their hearts. Indra saw this as a direct threat to his cherished position.

When we are too attached to position or material opulence, we become proud, and when someone threatens our status quo, we become territorial and angry and lose our sense of discrimination (Gita 2.63). That's what happened to Indra, and hence he behaved the way he did.

This display of Indra's anger is very instructive for us. We too may sometimes lose our centeredness and find fault with others, damaging their reputation. We may do this because we see others as our competition or better than ourselves. **This episode teaches us to keep our false ego and pride in check and practice humility.** In the end, that is what saved Indra from further problems. He bowed down to Krishna in humility, and Krishna forgave him.

The Almighty Krishna who is omnipresent and omnipotent is so humble then who are we in front of the God.

- Do we pride ourselves on our appearance, because Kamdev's the most beautiful God and nobody else can be that good.
- Is there a pride in our beauty. Remember, Goddess Lakshmi is the most lovely of them all and no one can be better than her.
- Are we proud of our wealth – Remember, Kuber is the richest God of all, and even the richest person on earth can't buy one city forget about other things.
- Are we proud of our knowledge - Remember, Goddess Saraswati is the wisest person on earth, and we don't know anything compared to her.
- Are you proud of our success or what we've accomplished? Nothing really.
- Are we proud of our body – Its ephemeral full of sweat, bile, phlegm, faeces, and urine.

Here is a story about Lord Vishnu a reincarnation of Krishna:

A famous incident goes like this: once, sages from different places had gathered on the banks of the Saraswati River. Unable to decide who was the greatest among the three—Lord Brahma, Lord Vishnu or Lord Shiva—the sages chose Bhrigu as their representative to test all the three deities and to decide as to who is the greatest.

He first went to Lord Brahma's abode. There he neither bowed in reverence nor greeted Lord Brahma. The Lord felt insulted but did not lose his temper.

After that Bhrigu went to Lord Shiva's place. Seeing Bhrigu approaching, Lord Shiva wanted to embrace him. But Bhrigu refused to accept Shiva's respect. At this Lord Shiva lost his temper and ran after him with his trident to kill him. Meanwhile Parvati came into the picture and Bhrigu was saved. Then, Bhrigu went to see Lord Vishnu. There he found Lord Vishnu in deep slumber. Seeing him, the preserver and sustainer of the world sleeping like an irresponsible person, Maharshi Bhrigu kicked Lord Vishnu on his chest. Lord Vishnu woke up as a result of the blow, bowed in reverence and said: "O Lord, be seated, I was not aware of your arrival, hence I could not welcome you. Forgive me! Your feet must be in pain as my chest is hard as 'Vajra' (mace)." Saying this, Lord Vishnu started pressing Bhrigu's legs and further said: "O Maharshi your footprint would remain on my chest forever as a sign of respect to you." This footprint of Bhrigu on Lord Vishnu's chest is known as srivatsa. After his return, Bhrigu narrated the whole story to the assembly of the sages.

Everyone concluded that it was Lord Vishnu who was the noblest and greatest among the trinity.

In the Bhagavad-gita Lord Krishna explains that we are part of a whole far bigger than ourselves: the all-attractive supreme, Krishna Himself. We have intrinsic self-worth because we are eternally loved by Him as His precious parts, irrespective of whether we succeed or fail in our endeavours. By humbly acknowledging that we are parts and not the whole, and by playing our role in a mood of devotional service, we can find inner security and satisfaction, thereby transcending the false ego's delusions.

"One of the most important rules of devotion is to consider oneself to be more insignificant than a blade of grass. When we consider ourselves to be important, we forget the significance of God. But when we remember how significant God is, then we realize our own insignificance. We are just one soul out of billions of souls on planet earth. The earth is just one planet out of billions of stars in the Milky Way galaxy and the Milky Way galaxy is just one out of billions of other galaxies in our universe.

My Guru taught me to practice self-surrender. He believed that the ego is the main obstacle to spiritual growth and that one must surrender the ego in order to attain enlightenment. This means letting go of the need to control and the need for self-aggrandizement and instead surrendering oneself to the will of God or a higher power. Self-surrender, according to Shree Kripalu Maharaj, is the process of relinquishing control over one's own life and entrusting oneself to God. This process involves a complete letting go of the ego and a willingness to submit to God's will.

It's admirable that we are taking the time to reflect on our behavior patterns and how they may be impacting ourselves and those around us. It's important to remember that we all have certain tendencies and habits, and it's okay to make mistakes and learn from them.

If you're noticing certain behaviors that may be harmful or unproductive, it's important to take steps towards changing them. This may involve seeking support from loved ones, speaking with a therapist or counselor, or simply practicing mindfulness and self-reflection on a regular basis.

It's also important to be kind and patient with yourself during this process. Change takes time and effort, but with dedication and determination, you can work towards becoming the best version of yourself. Remember, self-awareness is the first step towards personal growth and positive change.

"It is Nature that causes all movement. Deluded by the Ego, the fool harbors the perception that says, 'I Did it'." – Bhagvad Gita

In the next chapter we will talk about Negativity and how it crosses out the optimistic light in life.

8
Negativity

Overthinking is the biggest cause of unhappiness. The problem is rarely the problem. 99% of the harm is caused by us, in our heads. 1% of the harm is caused by reality, what happens and the outcome. Most of the time, the problem isn't the problem. The way we think about the problem is. The truth is, most problems aren't solved with more thinking, they are solved with less. We will find most answers we are looking for in silence, in timeband with a clear mind. If we can't solve a problem we should not try to.

Take my case. I am an emotional person, and I don't need to tell that to anyone. Anyone who's remotely familiar with me knows I'm low on emotional intelligence, and I don't have to try to show it. If I am livid, stressed, irritated, or unhappy, it just naturally shows on my face. Perhaps I ought to have been the last man in the world talking about handling emotions. But it seems to me that, having paid a high price for expressing my feelings, I know how they're going to work against us. **Louis Leo Holtz**, *an American former American football player, coach, and analyst said Don't tell your problem to people; eighty percent don't care, and the other twenty percent are glad you have them.*

Because of my inability to control my emotions, I've cut ties with my family, friends, colleagues, and relatives. People are judging me on what I'm saying and how I'm saying it, but they don't know my intentions. How can they? They're not God in the first place. I damage my reputation every time I'm losing control of my emotions. People get a lot of joy seeing me in misery. It's like a soap opera, full of drama, and a source of gossip.

There are so many times I have regretted losing my temper.

On the professional side, when arguing with a colleague in office, I stepped up to point out my position and wound up at the wrong end of the table. Although, I've been arguing the right thing. The colleagues thought of me as an impetuous man and somebody who would be easy to provoke. They're convinced that I can give them a response very easily. In addition, nobody empathized or sympathized while I became a talking point and laughingstock.

I've been known for being a socially awkward guy on the domestic front. Someone who doesn't think for a second before speaking. It's only because I am so upfront that I ruined relations with my family and friends. The reason is simple I am what I am on the face – straight forward. I have no way of hiding my feelings. People are not interested in hearing the truth; they're more interested in knowing the convenient truth. Something that would please them. Others who have ill will or bad intentions masquerade easily just because they can control their emotions. The fact is that people can be easily satisfied when they're able to hide their emotions.

These incidents may have diminished in the last few years but not vanished completely. Every time these experiences happen, I pledge to prevent it from happening again, but as they say it's easier said than done. With age I have become more mature but still my inherent nature doesn't deter me from controlling my emotions.

Upon self-examination, I realized it is due to the negativity that I am surrounded with. When I am in a negative state of mind, I tend to lose control and then one thing leads to another.

Ask yourself:

- Do I feel negative about something?
- Does it impact my thinking ability?
- Does it affect my decision-making ability?

Well obviously, we all feel negativity as we are humans, and it clouds our judgement.

People deal with all kinds of negativity. The reasons for feeling negative or stressed are endless. It ranges from our basic necessities like food, clothing, and shelter (Roti, Kapda and Makaan) to external factors like a death, an accident, a financial crisis, unemployment, incompatibility with a family member to internal factors like personal security, resources, health, friendship, intimacy, sense of belonging, respect, self-esteem, status, recognition, mental strength, and freedom.

These reasons are then manifested in various forms in our lives and affect us differently. Based on your EQ level, there is a difference in the degree of anxiety. To some it affects more while others are less influenced. It is also a matter of how we respond to a problem. For instance, when we're incompatible with our spouses, sisters, parents, and children, one partner is more affected by this than the other will be because of their differing responses.

I was unemployed for only a few months at the start of my career because I'd been square peg in round hole. After sitting home, without a job, I became demotivated which made me depressed. I made a promise when I got the job that I wasn't going to leave it anymore unless there was another job. Even now, the slightest of problems stresses me out and affects my mental health. The difference between now and then was that I was unmarried, and my father was alive to feed me then and now I am married and have no support from my father as he is no longer alive. When I look around, I see many people losing their jobs and facing a lot of difficulties in life, but they are handling the situation much better than me. They're running a family with the hardest problems, and they don't allow stress to affect their wisdom. Similarly, when I was going through the property dispute in my family after my father's demise my level of stress was way higher than my siblings which affected my mental health adversely and contributed to shaping my personality in a way that I never wanted. Moreover, when I was hurting, I bled on others.

It is not just about me, but we all get affected with negativity. Here are a few instances of people around me who deal with negativity in different ways:

I have seen two different couples dealing with infidelity in very contrasting ways. One pair thinks it's liberating and allows both of them to enjoy their life while the other couple goes through a horrible time in its lives that is just days away from breaking up. I don't imply the former couple is dealing with infidelity in an ideal way and the latter is dealing in not so ideal way but imagine both having kids at home and the effects of the second couple has on kids versus the first couple.

In his first year on the job, a colleague who had just started working at my place of employment had performed exceptionally well and had earned his due credit in the form of the best assessment. He had, however, suddenly deteriorated into a negative on account of his own expectations after the assessment. He felt that he was deserving of a different designation, compensation and greater powers which made him think about things in a new way. This has given rise to a full 360-degree transformation in his behavior. From being an excellent resource and asset for the company to becoming a total wreck and liability of the firm.

A friend I know is unhappy about not being able to own a car of her choice for quite some time although she already has a car to drive. It's a cause of stress in her life as she thinks she deserves an upgrade based on her status in society.

A friend is stressed due to the work pressure in the office. He starts his day at 7 AM in the morning and ends at 9 PM in the night. This hectic schedule leaves no time for family and friends and above all for himself. He whines about not having a good quality of life. Despite earning very well, he has a paucity of time. During the important years of his life when he should enjoy his life, he is busy running helter-skelter.

An ex-colleague I know is in extremely good stead financially, has a high paying job, a good house, a decent car, and everything that he could possibly wish for is stressed because he constantly compares his condition with his friends and wants to be better than them.

Likewise, there are so many examples around us where people are dealing with negativity in different ways. Some respond calmly while others make a fuss out of it. We need to understand the root cause of negativity. Why do we become negative in the first place?
We all know the answer, but we don't want to accept.

The simple answer is our desires. We all want good for us. We want:

- A good life.
- A good car.
- A good house.
- A good health.
- A good bank balance.
- A good daughter/son.
- A good wife/husband.
- Ohers to behave nicely with us.

While we want all this, we don't realize that everyone else wants the same for them. This is what gives rise to negativity.

When we expect:

- To control others.
- To love us sans our faults.
- Validation for our opinions and behavior.
- Love us unconditionally while we put conditions for them.
- Others to be available 24x7 physically, emotionally, and mentally while we are not available when they need us.

All of that can be traced to our desires. There's no limit to our desires. It's a function of our inherent drive to be in charge. We all want to control our surroundings to work to our advantage. That's not a bad thing because every person in the world needs it. Maybe some people are lucky that their surroundings work for them, but trust me, more than luck, it is the way they respond to situations. They've mastered the art of balancing emotions.

My Guru says: Desire means wishing for something. What do we wish for? There are five kinds of desires. Desire to see, hear, smell, taste, and touch. There are five sense organs that we have. All desires are related to these five senses. There cannot be a sixth one. If we abandon these five kinds of desires, we will automatically get rid of anger, greed, etc. We will become extremely peaceful.

The Gita says: We desire things related to what or whom we are attached to. Everyone has different desires because they are attached to different things and people. We can be attached to mother, father, children, spouse, wealth, fame, etc. We then develop desires according to these attachments.

The Vedas state, "Abandon all your desires and then worship God." Do not have worldly desires.

In the Bhagavada, Prahlada said to Lord Narasimha, "O Lord! You keep forcing me to ask for a boon, but I don't want anything since I am not a beggar. One who abandons all his desires, becomes equal to you. I don't desire anything.

There must be a reason why our mind gets attached to something? Yes, there is a reason. Constantly thinking that there is happiness in something leads to attachment to that thing. Thinking again and again that there is happiness there. This is causing us to get attached to that person or thing. That's it. This is the sole reason.

Constant Thinking!

- How does a human being become a Saint? Because of thinking.
- How does a human being go mad or take his own life? Because of the thoughts he has.

Our mind is such a great enemy of ours that it is the reason for everything we do. Your thoughts will result in what you become.

We human beings are selfish creatures. We associate and disassociate ourselves with others based on the level of benefits derived. We love people more when we get more benefits from them, and our love decreases/diminishes when the benefit derived is less or nonexistent. This is as simple as it gets. If we love someone and don't get the same attention or love, we stop loving them. We love and expect the most from our life partner, followed by our parents, children, siblings, neighbors, friends, extended family members and office colleagues. If we're not seeing these people behave in accordance with the norms of our anticipated behavior, then we start to imitate them through action and gesture.

Let's understand with the help of an example:

When a man is sick, he'd like his wife by his side to take care of him. If he's given the time, attention, and support of his wife, he'll do the same thing when she needs it. But he won't give it back in the same way if she doesn't support him. We'll continue to look at and judge the actions of people in our lives, and this will be driven by their behavior towards us.

Negativity is also the result of the state of our mind. We should try to keep ourselves unperturbed and calm in the toughest situations. Happiness is a choice. We always have the choice to be happy no matter the situation. In the worst situation, we can at least be happy that we are alive. Our mind is our best friend and our worst enemy. It all depends on what we allow into our mind. Our mind controls our actions, so we must be careful of what we allow in.

When the mind sends nothing but pessimistic messages, there are several ways to overcome this. Sometimes we just need some carbohydrates, but we also need to feed our consciousness the kinds of messages that strengthen our spiritual intelligence.

At the beginning of the Bhagvad-Gita, the world's greatest warrior, Arjuna, was overwhelmed with negative thoughts. He felt that he couldn't go on, and he wanted to withdraw from life.

Krishna gave him advice to lift him out of his bad mood. By appealing to his intelligence, Krishna reminded him that we are all eternal souls and we're naturally happy when we cooperate with the Supreme Self. Krishna told Arjuna all about the ultimate goal of life, which is to dedicate our lives to divine service, always think of the Supreme Person, and to return to the spiritual world.

After hearing from Krishna, Arjuna's bad mood completely lifted. He felt like himself again and was ready to charge into battle. We may not be warriors per se, but we've all experienced the rush of positive, creative energy that comes when we're released from the shackles of a bad mood. We see ourselves differently. We can see past our immediate troubles to where we want to be and what we want to accomplish in life.

Krishna's advice in the **Bhagavad-gita** is applicable in all situations. When we're going through stressful times, focusing on the cause of stress rarely helps us feel better.

If we remember simple rules to live life, we will be happier:

- Everyone leaves. Learn how to survive alone.
- The less we care, the happier we will be.
- Happiness is not about getting all we want; it is about enjoying all we have.
- If we can stay positive in a negative situation, we win.
- Stop expecting. Start accepting. Life becomes much easier.
- Worrying does not take away tomorrow's troubles, it takes away today's peace.

Ask yourself:

- Can I control my response to a situation?
- Will the outcome be different if I control my response?
- Would a better outcome make a difference in my relationship status?

Remember the difference between Anxiety and Trust:

Anxiety says: So many things could go wrong.
Trust says: I will focus my attention on what I can control.

Anxiety says: I need to micromanage the process.
Trust says: The universe is my collaborator.

Anxiety says: I feel like a failure.
Trust says: I'm still growing and learning.

Anxiety says: Everything is falling apart.
Trust says: May be a better plan is falling into place.

Anxiety says: I'm afraid of the unknown.

Trust says: Facing uncertainty expands my comfort zone.

Anxiety says: I need to have everything figured out.
Trust says: I'll figure out as I go.

The power of positive thinking can be understood from the below story from Bhagavad Gita:

"A king was touring his kingdom on his elephant. Suddenly he stopped in front of a shop in the market and said to his minister, "I don't know why, but I want to hang the owner of this shop." The minister was shocked. But before he could ask the king why, the king had moved on.

The next day, the minister went to that shop dressed as one of the locals to see the shopkeeper. He casually asked him how his business was faring. The shopkeeper, a sandalwood merchant, reported sadly that he had hardly any customer. People would come to his shop, smell the sandalwood and then go away. They would even praise the quality of the sandalwood but rarely buy anything. His only hope was that the king would die soon. Then there would be a huge demand for sandalwood for performing his last rites. As he was the only sandalwood merchant around, he was sure the king's death would mean a windfall.

The minister now understood why the king had stopped in front of this shop and expressed a desire to kill the shopkeeper. Perhaps, the shopkeeper's negative thought vibration had subtly affected the king, who had, in turn, felt the same kind of negative thought arising within.

The minister, a noble man, pondered over the matter for a while. Without revealing who he was or what had happened the day before, he expressed a desire to buy some sandalwood. The shopkeeper was pleased. He wrapped the sandalwood and handed it over to the minister.

When the minister returned to the palace, he went straight to the court where the king was seated and reported that the sandalwood merchant had a gift for him. The king was surprised. When he opened the package, he was pleasantly surprised by the fine golden colour of the sandalwood and its agreeable fragrance. Pleased, he sent some gold coins to the sandalwood merchant. The king also felt sorry in his heart that he had harboured unbecoming thoughts of killing the shopkeeper.

When the shopkeeper received the gold coins from the king, he was astounded. He began to proclaim the virtues of the king who had, through the gold coins, saved him from the brink of poverty. After some time, he recalled the morbid thoughts he had felt towards the king and repented for having entertained such negative thoughts for his own personal goal.

Moral of the story: If we have a good and kind thought for another person, that positive thought will come back to us in a favourable way. But if we harbour evil thoughts, those thoughts will come back to us as retribution.

Imagine you're holding a glass of water. If you hold it for a minute, it's no problem. If you hold it for 1 hour. You'll have an ache in your arm. If you hold it for a day, your arm will feel numb and paralyzed. The weight of the glass does not change, but the longer you hold it, the heavier it becomes. The stress & worries in life are like a glass of water. Think about them for a while. Nothing happens. Think about them for a bit longer, they begin to hurt. Think about them all day long, you'll feel paralyzed and incapable of doing anything.

There is no reason for us to carry the burden of stress in life. Whatever happens, happens for the best. We can't make any difference simply by thinking. It has to happen anyway.

Lesson from the Bhagavad Gita about negativity that we all must follow:

Change the way you think: Having positive thoughts helps us achieve a balanced perspective, stay confident, overcome negative notions, prepare well to meet challenges, and channelize your energy to achieve your goals. So, do not let negative thoughts take over your mind and ruin your chances. Being grateful, meditating, giving back to society, reading inspiring literature are a few practices that can help foster positive thoughts.

Stay calm: A calm mind will help us control our impulses, stay unperturbed and hopeful through both the good and the bad times, and keep stressors under control. It will also help us achieve clarity of thought, weigh our options, and channelize our energy towards gainful endeavours. The knowledge that changes is inevitable plays a big role in helping us stay calm.

My father's life was guided by this poem by **Norman McLeod**, and every time I felt negative in my life, he told me to follow it:

Courage, brother! do not stumble,
though your path be dark as night;
there's a star to guide the humble:
trust in God, and do the right.
Let the road be rough and dreary,
and its end far out of sight;
foot it bravely; strong or weary,
trust in God, and do the right.

My Guru taught me that, we cannot abandon desires. If we think about abandoning desire, it will increase even more, if we think about ending our animosity with someone, it will increase even more. How? For example, you try to think that you will forget your enemy. "I will forget my enemy. Who will I forget? Ramesh. Who is Ramesh? He is the one who caused me so much loss." And you will get angrier since that enemy will enter your mind. Your anger will not go away by doing this.

"No happiness exists here in this world. True Happiness only exists with God." Keep both these thoughts running in your mind constantly. Stop having worldly desires and instead start desiring God.

Our true desire is to attain complete Divine bliss, peace, happiness, etc. Our aim is to achieve that.

"You came in empty handed and you will leave empty handed. What is your today belonged to someone else yesterday and will belong to someone else tomorrow. So don't think much." – Bhagvad Gita

In the next chapter we will talk about happiness.

9
Happiness

There has been an unending debate on what is the true source of happiness. People of all age groups try to find answers in their own way.

- It makes a new-born kid happy to drink his mother's milk.
- The little boy feels happy to play with his toys.
- An adolescent feels happy trying to explore new & different things and wants to make a boyfriend or a girlfriend to be happy.
- A grown-up person wants to marry a smart, rich, and beautiful partner to be happy.
- A man who is married wishes to provide for his family with a high paying and steady job or business, which provides him with some sense of happiness.
- A middle-aged person's definition of happiness is a life with less liabilities and lesser stress.
- In the company of his grandchildren and in some cases in a higher calling, an old man finds comfort.

Not just the age, but different people have different meaning of happiness.

For some people, the key to happiness is money. Those kinds of people believe they can buy their happiness with money. With that logic, rich people shouldn't get upset because money should solve all of their problems. If that is the case, then why these so-called rich folks can't save the lives of their loved ones from serious illnesses. We've all seen what happened during Covid. In the face of adversity, it showed human frailty.

Even the richest of people who could afford the best of treatment after spending tons of money could not save their loved ones. There are only temporary problems that can be solved with money. Therefore, it can be assumed that money is not the source of happiness.

For some joy is the fulfilment of one's desire. These are people that do not enjoy fulfilment of just one desire. A person with a bicycle would, for instance, want to buy a scooter. The person who's driving his scooter wants a car. The owner of that little car wants to be able to buy a bigger one. The person with a bigger car wants to own a luxury car and this greed for having something better never ends. Its limitless. The owner of a luxury car doesn't like it because he wants a better car now. There's enough for need, but not for greed. There are no boundaries or limits to our desires. There is an infinite, boundless greed in us. For us, there can be no sufficient amount of wealth and material entitlement. Money's enough to give us our momentary satisfaction, which fades as time goes by. As a result, it can be safely assumed that fulfilment of material desires is not the source of happiness.

If not, money and desire then is it success that is the source of happiness?

Success means a lot of things in different forms and definitions, so it is hard to understand or comprehend at once. For a variety of people success means something else entirely.

It is believed by some that success lies in having enough money. We thought money was the key to success when we were kids. We'd have been happy if we had the money. It's only when we're grown up that we realize how hard it is to make money, and that it takes away everything else. This is peace of mind, friendship, relationships, and quality of life. If success means money and having money that doesn't have the abovementioned characteristics, it's not success, it's an illusion of success. We spend our entire life running after money and in the end, we take nothing with us. **According to Arnold H. Glasow –**"*Success is simple. Do what's right, the right way, at the right time.* So, this implies that having money is not success and it is not a source of happiness.

For some, occupying a position of authority signifies success, and the sense of power derived from it brings happiness. Let's hypothetically consider that the happiest individual is the most powerful person; by that reasoning, India's Prime Minister would be presumed the happiest as the most influential figure in the country. However, this assumption doesn't hold true. Neither wealth nor power possesses the ability to prevent the loss of loved ones; fate ultimately determines life's course. When our time is up, no amount of wealth, influence, or the best medical care can save us. The notion that the Prime Minister would find joy in spending quality time with family, leisurely travel, or material acquisitions is also misguided. The demands of national duties limit personal time and leisure activities, respect stems from the position held—transient and not intrinsic, and spending is constrained by the responsibility to allocate public funds judiciously. Additionally, the Prime Minister is subject to constant scrutiny from various quarters including the media, opposition, and the public. Furthermore, power tends to create an illusory sense of success. It's the position itself that commands respect, not necessarily the individual. Retired civil servants often note a shift in how people perceive them post-retirement, realizing that those who once sought their attention now seem to have disappeared. From these observations, it becomes evident that power is not a source of genuine success or happiness.

Let's understand this with the help of an example:

There was a minister once who had a son. The son fell gravely ill and needed immediate attention. He wanted to take his son to the hospital, but the son didn't have the strength to go to the hospital. The Minister then telephoned the doctor and asked if he'd be interested in visiting his son at home. The doctor's agreed, leaving all his patients to take care of his son. He's been seeing his son for urgent medical care and prescribing him medicines. The minister turned into an ordinary person after a couple of years and declared bankruptcy. He's got a sickness and needs to be looked after immediately. He called a doctor to come see him at home when he was bed ridden. This time, the doctor knew that the Minister was no longer in power and no longer rich and powerful. He knew that he wouldn't get any favours, and maybe not even be compensated equivalent to the opportunity cost of diagnosing a different patient at the same time and hence decided to not go.

Moral of the story: It was the position that made the doctor do things out of the way and not the person. This proves that power is not the source of happiness.

For some, fame brings happiness and success. Is it famous people who don't lose their loved ones, or are they always happy? No, that's not the truth. The famous, too, don't get immunity and have a lot of other reasons to be unhappy. They're always jealous and insecure about losing their fame. Reaching the top is no easy task, but it's challenging to stay there. Take the example of Rajesh Khanna, legendary star of the olden days who didn't want to admit that his fame was fading. After his golden years had passed, he could never come to terms that he was no more a superstar and rejected sub-par and inferior roles which didn't show him as a protagonist. For many years he had remained a mystery to the public, and then finally met his fate. The most famous people are the loneliest. The soul is not satisfied by fame. Fame doesn't fulfil the soul. It fills artistic craving. Therefore, we can say being famous doesn't guarantee happiness.

Then what exactly is Happiness, if not Money, Fulfilment of Desire, and Success (Money, Power, & Fame)

Ask yourself:

- What makes me happy?
- Is it money, success, power?

Happiness doesn't mean the same to everyone.

Let's understand through an example of a priest and an alcoholic how it is different for both at the same time.

When a bottle of wine is lying in front of a brahmin priest and an alcoholic man, they both look at it in different ways. The sheer sight of the wine bottle annoys the priest, and he doesn't want to touch the bottle for it will destroy his dharma while on the other hand, the alcoholic man couldn't resist to open the bottle for he is dying to consume it. If a bottle of wine is a source of happiness, it should have the same effect on both, but it's not the bottle of wine that's the source of happiness, it's the outlook of two different people toward happiness. It was a source of hate to one, and happiness to the other.

Happiness means different to different people at different times.

- A starved person says: I feel happy when fed.
- A rich person says: I feel happy to have more money.
- A fat person says: I feel happy at losing weight.
- A thin person says: I feel happy at gaining weight.
- A person with good heart says: I feel happy when appreciated for good nature.
- A beautiful person says: I feel happy when appreciated for outer beauty.
- An alcoholic person says: I feel happy drinking alcohol.
- A teetotaller says: I feel happy not drinking alcohol.
- A good leader says: I feel happy nurturing more leaders under me.
- A parent says: I feel happy seeing my child growing up and succeeding in life.
- A teacher says: I feel happy seeing my pupil achieving success.
- A spiritual guru says: I feel happy seeing my disciples leading a life of righteous path.
- A poor person says: I feel happy to have a roof on my head, clothes to wear and food to eat.
- A coffee lover says: A cup of coffee in the coffee shop in the middle of work gives me happiness.

But sadly, the irony is that all these ways of finding happiness could have very well been said by a person in Ukraine a few months ago, who is facing a life and death situation now. It is an example happening right in front of our eyes, to show the ephemeral nature of material happiness. Even if the loss of happiness is not as drastic as in Ukraine or faced by a person with a sudden diagnosis of a terminal illness, the fact is that material happiness eventually always gets lost. For example, if a cup of coffee gives you happiness, the fact is that one cup of coffee will certainly not give you everlasting happiness. Having more cups of coffee will in fact make you throw up instead of giving you more happiness.

Ask yourself:

- Do I really know my source of happiness?
- Do I confuse happiness with temporary pleasures?

I asked the same question to myself, and this is what I came up with:

- When I was a kid, I used to think, I will be happy when I finish school.
- As I grew up, I thought, I will be happy when I'm married.
- After getting married, I thought, I will be happy when I buy a bigger house.
- After buying a bigger house, I thought, I will be happy when I get a better job.
- My next target to be happy is when my kid will grow older, and I will retire.
- One day, I will retire, and all the time will be gone, and I will think now I can't be happy.

Let us try to understand with the help of a story:

One day, a rich dad took his son on a trip to a village. He wanted to show him how poor someone can be. They spent time on the farm of a poor family. On their return from the trip, the father asked his son, "How was the trip?" "It was great, Dad". Did you see how poor people live?" the father asked. "Oh yes," said the son. "So, tell me, what did you learn from the trip?" asked the father. The son answered: We have one dog, they have four, we have a pool, they have rivers, we have tube-lights at night, they have stars, we buy foods, they grow theirs, we have walls to protect us, they have friends. We have television, they spend time with family and relatives. The boy's father was speechless. Then his son added: "Thanks, Dad for showing me how poor we are."

Moral of the story is, it is not about money that makes us rich, its simplicity, love, compassion, friendships, values, family that makes our lives rich.

This led me to the conclusion that we can define happiness as something which is:

- A comfortable state of life.
- Being in the present moment.
- Gratitude for what we have.
- A positive attitude towards life.

- Achieving goals that matter to us.
- Achieving happiness in the truest sense by living in the moment.

But how do we ensure a good "state of mind"?

- By Being Tolerant
- By Ensuring lowliness
- By Inculcating Humility
- By Ignoring negative thoughts
- By Being Patient

How do we ensure to live in the present moment?

- Stop thinking about past glories.
- Stop thinking about bad memories.
- Appreciating what is happening now in our life.
- Stop worrying about future.

How do we feel gratitude towards life?

- Appreciate small things in life.
- Appreciate the good in everyone.
- Appreciate the good memories we have collected.
- Detaching the value of pleasure from external things.
- Stop comparing ourselves with people who have achieved more in life.
- Start seeing how our life is better than so many people below us.

How do we ensure positivity?

- Stop feeling like a victim.
- Learn to control ourselves and not the environment around us.
- We can choose to be positive by thanking God for everything we have.
- Surround ourselves with everything positive; what we see and what we hear.

How do we achieve goals in life?

- Knowing true purpose in life.

- Learn new skills and improve upon existing ones.
- Make a mindset shift; what we think and believe is what we act upon.
- Avoid activities that negatively impact our life and hinder our success.
- Design our environment for success; be with the people who are right for us.
- Doing a life audit; figure out where do we stand in life; health, finances, personal development, relationship, career, self-care, home life and free time.

How do we feel happy in the truest sense?

- Find our true calling, our purpose in life.
- Love what we do, do what we love.
- See God in every living being.
- Eliminate negativity around us.

Most importantly we need to have faith in God. Whatever happens it happens for good.

All these virtues are intrinsic in nature. We can't change our surroundings, but we can change ourselves. Change starts from within. Our mind is a magnet, if we think of blessings, we attract blessings, if we think of problems, we attract problems. Always cultivate good thoughts and remain positive.

As per Krishna, there are three types of happiness.

In Chapter 18, Verse 36 Sri Krishna says to Arjun,

*"sukham tv idanim tri-vidham shrinu me bharatarshabha
abhyasad ramate yatra duhkhantam cha nigachchhati"*

Translation:

"And now hear from me, O Arjun, of the three kinds of happiness in which the embodied soul rejoices and can even reach the end of all suffering."

First Happiness:

Satvik or Pure happiness: It is the happiness that arises from the elevation of the soul. However, attaining this is not easy. One pursuing satvik or pure happiness must practice a lot of discipline. That is why, it feels like poison in the beginning but nectar in the end.

*"yat tad agre viham iva pariname mitopamam
tat sukham sattvikam proktam atma-buddhi-prasada-jam"*

Translation:

"That which seems like poison at first, but tastes like nectar in the end, is said to be happiness in the mode of goodness. It is generated by the pure intellect that is situated in self-knowledge."

Bhagavad Gita, Chapter 18, Verse 37

Second Happiness:

Rajasik or result-oriented happiness: This is the materialistic pleasure that is derived when the senses meet external objects that create a feeling of gratification. However, this kind of happiness is temporary.

*vishayendriya-sanyogad yat tad agre mritopamam
pariname visham iva tat sukham rajasam smritam"*

Translation:

"Happiness is said to be in the mode of passion when it is derived from the contact of the senses with their objects. Such happiness is like nectar at first but poison at the end."

Bhagavad Gita, Chapter 18, Verse 38

Third Happiness:

Tamasic or slothful happiness: This is the lowest form of happiness and is derived from sleeping or being lazy. The soul is never nurtured through these practices yet since there is a tiny sense of pleasure asscciated with it, people wrongfully consider it to be a state of happiness.

"yad agre chanubandhe cha sukham mohanam atmanah
nidralasya-pramadottha tat tamasam udahritam"

Translation:

*"That happiness which covers the nature of the self from beginning to end,
and which is derived from sleep, indolence, and negligence, is said to be in the
mode of ignorance."*

Now that we have learnt about the different kinds of happiness, it is
up to us to decide, what kind of happiness is desirable for us:

- temporary happiness, or
- freedom from miseries with a chance of falling from that pedestal, or
- attainment of the bliss of the impersonal form of God.

There is no doubt that there is happiness in the world and that
happiness does not last. It satisfies the senses for a short time and
ultimately fades away, leading us to feel miserable yet again. That's why
material happiness is named as the illusion of happiness.

As per my Guru, there is a fourth type of happiness which is the:

"Bliss attained by conscious mind from All Conscious God".

Here the divine mind meets the divine beloved (God) in its full
consciousness. This bliss is supreme and even a tiny drop of this bliss is
far more potent than if you were to multiply Brahmanand (bliss of
impersonal form of God) with 100 quadrillion (1 followed by 17 zeroes).
This bliss is also ever increasing, ever-new and ever-lasting. There is
nothing bigger than this bliss, so the chance of seeing something better
and losing interest in this is not possible.

So, this is the happiness that we truly seek. Even though we have
attained the first two kinds of happiness countless times, we have never
been satisfied since that is not our true desire. We have never attained
the third type of happiness which leads to neither pain nor pleasure. But
this does not meet the goal.

Bhagavad Gita, Chapter 18, Verse 39.

One can derive true happiness only by achieving a peaceful state of mind. There is no greater happiness than the happiness one gets from being at peace with oneself and being one with God.

Let us think for a moment and ponder on a couple of questions.

- Do you like it when happiness derived from objects fades away?
- Do you like it when the newness of things is gone, and it feels like "same old same old"?
- Do you have anything so great, wonderful, and satisfying that you would not even consider something superior?

My Guru taught me that the ultimate goal of our life, is to find true, everlasting happiness, God has left the choice on us to choose any of the above four forms of happiness. The wise ones do not settle for anything less than what they truly desire!

Choose your happiness wisely!

"The key to happiness is the reduction of desires." – Bhagvad Gita

In the next chapter we will talk about Love which is important to be happy.

10

Love

The human species is the most selfish of them all. Ever wondered why? We're always expecting something back when we do something for someone. So, we give and accept, which means a feeling of giving is conditional. Every action that targets someone else is meant to get something in return. We love to be loved, we care to be cared, we pamper to be pampered, we detest to be abhorred. Don't believe me. Introspect and you will realize what I am saying is true that you, me, and us, we all are selfish. Is it ever occurred to you that, when we love someone madly and do not receive the same love in return, how are we feeling? Devastated and dejected. It's not possible for us to force someone to love us. We're expecting them to be natural lovers. But if our thoughts don't match, our mental wavelength don't match we don't feel it.

Let's take a look at the love marriage case. The same couple, who were willing to do whatever for each other prior to the wedding, don't feel that way once they get married. The real feelings began to surface the first day they had moved together under one roof and were better acquainted. The love on day one would not be the same after one year and change drastically after a few years. Because when they first started seeing each other, they were in awe with each other. They've seen everything that they want to see, which is outside beauty, happy habits, a good nature, and ignoring all of the others. They became aware of each other's compatibility and changed as they spent more time together. Somewhere in that journey, love was lost, and more priorities began to take over the relationship. If we're not getting what we want, be that love, care, or attention, how do we change our behaviour depending on the degree of loving, caring and attentiveness to a loved one? We stop calling when a friend doesn't call, even though we want to talk, assuming that the friend doesn't care, so why should we care? Forget about love, when we hate someone, we do things to hurt them. What do we get from it? It's a pleasure for our sadistic senses. That's the reason I said all of us are self-centred.

Why are we selfish?

Do you think it gives us pleasure to be selfish? What does that even mean? How selfishness can be a blessing to anyone in the world. I must be out of mind to say that. No, I've not lost my mind. All right, I'm going to try to explain it in a different way. How come we're looking for happiness? Why do we want to be happy? Because it is natural to us. Expecting the best in every situation is selfishness. We all want to feel happy with every action we take.

Ever wondered what makes us cry after we've been born to this world; the logical answer is that tears make us happy. We enter the world of light when we've survived nine months in our mother's black womb, and as soon as we can look at a new environment, we begin to see it. At this point, we don't know how to react, and the only comforting response is to cry. In other words, we are making ourselves happy by our natural reaction which is crying at that time. On the contrary when a mother gives birth to a baby, the sound of the baby's cry gives her happiness. Because it is the proof of the baby's existence. She would start to cry if she didn't hear the cry. She expresses her happiness in both cases by joy and sorrow. In both the cases it is normal for her to be happy.

If we're starving, what are we going to do? We eat. What's going to happen after we eat? We're able to satisfy our hunger. We feel so happy when we've settled our hunger. It does the same thing when we're out of water. We quench our thirst and feel happy. Likewise, there are so many things we do that give us joy such as playing, working, sleeping. Let us say, for the sake of discussion, that playing keeps us fit. It's true, but if we all know it keeps us fit, why don't everyone play when they feel like playing and others are happy doing something else? And what's the matter with work? Isn't working making us happy as well? Given a choice no one wants to work, but you see working is not a choice, it's a necessity. We work to earn. We earn to make ends meet. So that we can have food to eat, clothes to wear and a roof on our head to live. While we ensure all this the ultimate objective which is getting fulfilled is that of happiness. Some people don't work at all. What do they do then? Beg. If begging instead of working keeps them happy, so be it. They are better off not working. They feel happy not working. Sleeping we all know is important for our health. Even when someone in the family is seriously ill, we don't miss our sleep. We would ignore the worst of problems in the world just to have a good night's sleep. Because we are selfish creatures. When we feel sad, we cry, when in pain we agonize, we feel angry we yell, we feel jealous, we gossip, when we get good news, we feel excited, when we get bad news, we go silent. All these are natural reactions in different situations ultimately fulfilling our selfish desire to be happy.

Well, we're going to dig a bit deeper. Let us take a look at the underlying principle of happiness. Why all of us are looking for happiness and why are we akin to want our best in everything. Maybe we're all part of a common identity. That's the identity we all belong to. Is this part of a larger thing? Let us imagine, for a moment, we are part of an all-encompassing, omnipresent, omnipotent, most powerful God in the world. The God is bound to happiness or in other words God is synonymous to happiness. What it means is that we are selfish because we want happiness for us, we want happiness because we are part of God. To make it simple, another name for happiness is God. It is thus proven that, by being a part of God, we are in our natural nature to be selfish. To find the best in everything we do is natural to us.

You know every soul is looking for some kind of happiness either consciously or unconsciously. Even then when someone calls us selfish, we feel bad and retaliate. When everyone wants to ensure the best for themselves, then why do we feel bad when we are accused of being selfish. We go out of our way to defend ourselves to prove that we are not selfish. Important to note here is to have the knowledge that it's "you" and "me" who are selfish. Not "only you" and "only me". The day we understand this that everyone wants their best, we will stop fighting and start loving.

There are two parties to every transaction, a buyer, and a seller. The seller wants to negotiate the best price for his goods and services he is providing, while the buyer wishes to ensure that they are being sold at a fair price. Eventually they both settle on a mutually agreed price which is in the best interests of each other. It is a win for both sides. If they do not agree on a price, there will be no trading. We should draw an analogy from this and see life through the prism of a trade deal. Sometimes, there is an agreement and sometimes there is a disagreement. Being selfish isn't a bad thing. We should fill our cup before trying to pour into everyone else's.

The Saints know where their true selfishness lies. It is in being close to God and so they seek happiness by detaching themselves from the world.

How is selfishness connected with love?

How does this relate to love? As self-centred beings, we often anticipate that when we love someone, they should reciprocate in precisely the same manner. If we don't receive the expected love in return, our affection tends to diminish, and in certain instances, it even fades away. As I've previously outlined, our love often comes with attached conditions, expecting the person to conform to our desired actions and behaviours.

Let's understand with an example:

A dad is asking his son, 'Dear son, can I have a glass of water?' The son quickly gets up fills a glass with water and gives it to his father and says, 'Dad here you go'. His father believes that he's blessed to have such a loyal son. The dad is calling again after a while, Dear son, can you give me my reading glasses? Son doesn't get up this time. The father is shouting again, son, I want you to pass my glasses. The son ignores the call. The father asks the third time, and the son doesn't respond. After repeatedly asking his son for the glasses and not getting it, the father this time feels angry and whispers how unlucky I am to have a son like devil.

Moral of the story is that it's not the son who was the source of happiness to the father, it's the selfishness derived from the son that gave him a sense of happiness. When the son behaved as per expectations of the father, he was happy and when against his expectations, he was angry. On the basis of other people's behaviour, our emotions change a lot in a day. Our love vacillates many times in the same day.

When faced with the imminent loss of someone dear, our initial reaction typically revolves around concerns about our own future. We worry about how we'll manage without them, who will fill their role, and how we'll cope. These thoughts often centre around our own well-being. However, ideally, our focus should shift towards contemplating the person themselves.

Is this love? No, it is trade. Any relationship which is based on give and take is trade.

So, what defines genuine love? It's the act of selflessly doing everything for your loved ones, devoid of any expectations in return – that is love. The purest form of love is unconditional, resembling the bond between a mother and her child, where love flows without any demands. Regardless of a child's actions, a mother's love remains unwavering. It's crucial for us to adopt this philosophy in life, loving unconditionally without anticipating anything in return. This altruistic approach is challenging in our world, but by making small efforts, we can strive to reshape it, creating a more beautiful place to live.

This means:

- Where there are only expectations, it is selfishness.
- Where there is give and take, it is trade.
- Where there is only giving, it is love.

Love fills you with gratitude, positivity, affection, and care. No action or gesture gives you the satisfaction of completeness. Even after doing everything for your beloved, you feel a sense of discontent as if you have not done enough.

Until this point, our upbringing has instilled in us a particular definition of love. This definition encompasses feelings of infatuation, attachment, and care. While these words sound appealing, grasping their true essence remains challenging. They are often coupled with expectations, making it nearly impossible to comprehend them fully. In our perception, these words inevitably intertwine with the notion of expectation; without it, relating to any of these concepts becomes arduous.

Modern-day love has taken on a different, more toxic form. It's reached a point where people are willing to resort to extreme measures, even death, in the name of love. Tragically, numerous lives are lost due to honour killings orchestrated by family members. Instances of suicide occur when individuals are unable to attain the affection of their desired partner. Shockingly, some resort to horrific acts like acid attacks or other forms of violence against their beloved. Regrettably, certain movies romanticize such destructive expressions of love.

Ask yourself:

- What is my definition of love?
- Do I expect from the people I love?
- Do I love them unconditionally?

This is exactly I used to feel about love. For me love was about taking and expecting. I always expected my loved one's to behave according to my requirements. Be it my father, wife, kid, and siblings.

My Guru changed my perspective towards love. As per my Guru, Love has a definition which consist of 4 aspects.

First aspect: It must be गुण-रहितम् which means the lover must not see the qualities of the beloved.

There is a story of a girl named Yogasheela in the Puranas. Yogasheela was very beautiful. One day a king saw her as he was riding. He told her father that he wanted her. The father was poor. And the king was not cultured. It would be dangerous to give him his daughter. But if he did not obey, the king would kill them both. The daughter said, "Father, tell him to come back in a month." The king agreed to return in a month, and he posted his military in that village so they wouldn't escape. Through yoga, she dried up her body such that she was just skin and bones. Even her face had shrunk to her skull. The king came and asked for her. The father brought her in. When he saw her, he said, "Not this one, bring the one I saw that day." The father said, "My lord, she is the same girl, my only daughter. She fell ill. The king fled without looking back because he only loved her beauty. Without that beauty, to hell with the girl. He didn't want a bag of bones. Even in the world no one would accept.

Just like when a tree bears fruits, flocks of birds come without being called. And when the fruits fall, all the birds leave without being chased away! Such is the world and its love. Today you love someone for their quality, tomorrow that quality is gone.

We all love someone for their quality, but can we love someone without it? The answer is No.

Second aspect: It must be कामना-रहितम् which means Don't love your Beloved with selfish desires. Otherwise, the love will end if our desires are not fulfilled.

When we attach material desires to our loved ones and those desires are not fulfilled, we stop loving the person. Every now and then, we read news about partners leaving their spouses because the other partner committed to fulfil something but couldn't fulfil it. A man promised his girlfriend that he would buy a Mercedes car if she agreed to marry him. After they got married, he couldn't afford to buy the car and she deserted him. A man promised to provide his wife a minimum amount as monthly expenses but couldn't provide, so his wife abandoned him. While this may not be applicable for everyone, but we tend to put conditions on our love and based on the fulfilment of those conditions our love increases and decreases.

Let's understand with a story:

A very poor man lived with his wife. One day, his wife, who had very long hair asked him to buy her a comb for her hair to grow well and to be well groomed. The man felt very sorry and said no. He explained that he didn't even have enough money to fix the straps of his watch he had just broken. She didn't insist on her request. The man went to work and passed by a watch shop, sold his damaged watch at a low price, and went to buy a comb for his wife. He came home in the evening with the comb in his hand ready to give his wife. He was surprised when he saw his wife with a very short haircut. She had sold her hair and was holding a new watch band. Tears flowed simultaneously from their eyes, not for the futility of their actions, but for the reciprocity of their love. They both loved each other without any selfish desires.

Third Aspect: प्रतिक्षणवर्धमानम् which means the love for our beloved should increase with every passing moment.

This isn't true in our material world because in both the above instances we have put conditions on our loved ones.

Let's take the example of a married couple.

In the initial years of our marriage we love our partners so much that we pamper them a lot. We take care of what they eat, what they wear, how they feel, and a lot of other aspects but after a few years of marriage we ignore all of this. Our attitude changes from being 'I am there for my partner' to 'he/she" will take care of himself/herself'. Once we compared our wife with the beauty of Taj Mahal and now we don't even want to go to Taj Mahal. The basic condition of love is that it should increase with time and even after giving everything we should feel that we have not done enough.

Fourth Aspect: अनुभवरूपम which means the love for our beloved can only be felt.

When a mute person eats a sweet dish and loves it, he feels really good after eating it but can't express it in words. Love can't be expressed in words, it can only be felt. The voiceless person can't express what he feel about the sweet but knows they love it. Similarly, when we love someone deeply, we know it how we feel about that person and words can;t express our feelings.

Our glorious religion is full of the definition of Love. As per Bhagavad Gita, Love has different definition. They are:

1. **Universal Love:** The Bhagavad Gita teaches us the concept of universal love, emphasizing that love should be extended to all beings without any discrimination. It encourages individuals to embrace an expansive and inclusive love that transcends boundaries of caste, creed, gender, or nationality. This love recognizes the inherent divinity in all beings and treats them with respect and compassion.

2. **Detachment in Love**: The Bhagavad Gita emphasizes the importance of practicing love without attachment to the outcome. It suggests that love should be selfless and free from expectations. By cultivating a sense of detachment, individuals can experience love in its purest form, without being driven by desires, possessiveness, or the need for reciprocity.

3. **Love as a path to union with the divine:** The Bhagavad Gita teaches that love can be a powerful means to attain union with the divine. It suggests that when individuals direct their love towards a higher spiritual reality, such as the supreme being or the universal consciousness, they can experience a profound sense of oneness and transcendence. Love becomes a path for spiritual growth and realization.

4. **Love as Sacrifice:** The Bhagavad Gita teaches that love often involves sacrifice and selflessness. It encourages individuals to act in the best interest of others, even if it requires personal sacrifice. True love is not driven by selfish motives but is willing to give and serve without expecting anything in return. This selfless love helps individuals cultivate virtues such as humility, compassion, and generosity.

5. **Love as a Duty:** The Bhagavad Gita teaches emphasizes the importance of fulfilling one's duties with love and devotion. It suggests that love can be expressed through the performance of one's responsibilities and obligations in life. By approaching our duties with a loving attitude, we contribute to the welfare of society and foster harmonious relationships with others.

Let's try to find the true meaning of love.

Let us not expect our beloved to behave how we want them to behave, let us not put conditions for love, let us not love them for their qualities, and our selfish desires. The day we do this, we will know the true meaning of love. Love can conquer the world.

"He who had no attachments can really love others. For his love is pure and divine." – Bhagvad Gita

In the next chapter we will talk about Karma which ensures mindful thoughts & actions.

11

Karma

Hinduism identifies karma as the relationship between a person's mental or physical action and the consequences following that action. It also signifies the consequences of all the actions of a person in their current and previous lives and the chain of cause and effect in morality.

In Buddhism, karma refers to the principle of cause and effect. The result of an action — which can be verbal, mental, or physical — is not determined by not only the act but also the intention.

The sum of a person's good and bad actions in this and previous states of existence, viewed as affecting their future.

As the common sayings "what goes around comes around" and "what you sow is what you reap" are great examples of how karma works.

We have a choice to earn good karma by doing good deeds and bad karma by doing bad deeds. There are references for good and bad deeds in our religious books should we choose to live a righteous life. But the path is extremely challenging, one filled with hardships and sacrifices. Most of us don't choose to follow that path, while some of us try to follow it, but end up quitting it. In today's world of impatience, zero tolerance and short term gains we can't lead of life of hardships. So, we choose an alternative path. As far as we're concerned, Karma is defined in our own terms. We're interpreting it according to our convenience and needs. Whatever suits us fits in the definition of good karma and whatever doesn't suit us fit in the definition of bad karma. For example, it's good karma for some people to eat nonvegetarian food because it reduces Earth's burden, whereas it's bad karma for vegetarians to eat non-vegetarian food. Alcohol consumption to some people is a source of achieving nirvana and for some it's a peccadillo. When a thief steals material things, it is regarded as a sin, but when someone steals someone else's trust, it is normal.

Ask yourself:

- What is my definition of Karma?
- Is my definition of Good and Bad Karma same as that of others?

I did some soul searching and realized that my definition of karma suits me more than but it not towards the righteous path. A small example is that I enjoyed gossiping about others, talk bad about them. It was so convenient for me to think that it is the right thing to do. But later I realized that finding fault in someone else is the biggest proof of one's own faults. When we point one finger towards others three fingers are pointed towards us. We are full of vices like Lust, Anger, Greed, attachments and so on then how can we find fault in other?

As per my Guru, there are 6 types of people. They are:

- Those who want to do bad for others at their own expense. They want to do bad for others even if it means bad for them. They're the worst humans on earth.
- Those who want to do bad for others for their benefit. They are better than the worst kind but second worse kind of people.
- They're the ones who want to do good for themselves, and they're the ones who want to do good for everybody else. In order, they're superior to the other two classes and third class.
- Those who don't wish bad for others for their own benefit. They're not going to harm other people for their own sakes. The fourth kind is better than the other three types of people.
- Those who only wish good for others. These are the second-best type of people.
- Those who want good for others at their own expense. They'll be good for others, even if it's bad for them. They're the finest people in the world. They're saints most of the time. They're real spiritual disciples of God.

Most of us fall within the first four categories. We're often blinded by our arrogance, perceiving ourselves as greater than even God. Erroneously, we assume that greatness can be achieved solely through the support of others. Secondly, we make the mistake of believing that we're capable of achieving greatness independently. Consequently, we completely overlook the presence of God, effectively demonstrating our lack of belief in it.

Is it our actions that define our deeds or is it our intentions that define it?

Let us understand it with the help of a story:

Once there lived a king who was very generous. Every day he used to give alms to poor and needy Brahmins. One day as usual, he was giving away food to the Brahmins. At the same time, an eagle flew above. It was carrying a dead snake. A few drops of poison fell into the vegetable bowl. Vegetable from the same bowl was served to the Brahmins. Neither the King nor the Brahmins knew about this and the Brahmins ate the food and died.

Chitragupta who is responsible for Karma got confused after seeing this and wondered who is responsible for the death of Brahmins

He can't write it off on the snake as the snake was killed already
He can neither write on the eagle as the eagle was carrying its prey
He can't write off on the king as the king was a generous man and had no knowledge of the poisoned food

He went to consult Lord Yama about this. Lord Yama told him " Don't worry Chitragupta. The time is already ripe, and you will know very soon on whose account you should write off the sins of the Brahmin being killed."

On the same day, three Brahmins came to the city where the King lived. But they didn't know the way to the palace. So, they saw a potter woman and asked her the way. The potter woman clearly showed them the way but added " Be Careful O! Brahmins. If you eat the food given by the King, you may get killed." The Brahmins were shocked and returned without meeting the King.

On seeing this event, Dharmaraja immediately told Chitragupta to write the bad deeds in the account of the potter woman for speaking a lie and blaming the king without knowing the true reality.

This story tells that Karma is not just accounted for the actions we do. An action done with good intention might even harm someone without the knowledge of the doer as the world is full of strange coincidences.

As humans many a times we believe in rumours and become a messenger unknowingly spreading a lie.

The real culprit is not the king, the eagle, or the snake. It is all of us who are spreading the lies without knowing the truth!

The intention of a crime is always examined by our judicial system when it comes to court. The most severe penalties are imposed when a crime has been committed with malicious intent, but in the event of an offence arising out of defence it is considered to be mild and mostly decided on behalf of the accused. If our God and the system of law are looking at intentions, why can't we take a similar approach to Karma? We are constantly judging people around us based on their actions and pass the verdict. Who are we to decide about good and bad deeds without knowing the true intentions. We don't have the ability to read others' thoughts. We are mortal beings with limited reasoning capacities, but we don't shy away a second from accusing other people of crimes without reflection on our actions.

We're always lying, we're hiding things, we're deceiving, we're talking bad about people, and we assume nobody's going to know. We even lie to and cheat our own spouses and keep things in private trying to hide from them thinking they wouldn't know but in our heart, we know we are lying, deceiving, and hiding. That's a common practice among the majority of partners. This behaviour has been normalized, and we don't think it's a bad thing. Forget about feeling, we don't even remotely know that it is a bad deed. We're just saying that physical actions are bad if we don't know the motive for them.

It is already established above that our intentions decide good and bad Karma rather than words or actions. For example, when you help someone in need, the action leaves an imprint, and as these imprints develop with experiences, it opens the possibility of you receiving help in return when you need it. Conversely, harmful actions bring about negative consequences — you won't receive help when you need it, but instead, you may be harmed.

Karma psychology is essentially the same. If you act with good intentions, happiness will follow. If you act with ill intentions, problems will follow.

When you see dishonest and cruel people in positions of power get ahead in life or kind people face hardships and die young, it may be hard for you to believe in karma. Many people invest in karma only in times of distress or when uncontrollable situations occur, such as a decline in health.

Karma often helps people cope with these situations. Even people who don't believe in karma often think that good deeds lead to a good outcome.

However, there is a downside to this belief. Some people are selfless givers, who think their good deeds and sacrifices will help them win in life. But many of these givers also fail because they find it hard to set boundaries when helping others. They may drop their ambitions and goals to help others, making them fall behind in life.

Karma has four main principles:

- **Small actions can lead to great results:** The smallest action can bring about immense happiness or great sadness. What you may consider a small act of goodwill might be huge for another in the same way that a short hurtful remark can have a lasting impact on them. You might not realize it but doing good deeds for others — no matter how small — might be life-changing for them.
- **Karma is nontransferable:** That is, you're responsible for your own karmic experiences. No one else can experience your karma for you nor can they remove it for you and vice versa.
- **Noncommitted actions** won't give you the results you want. You must fully commit to actions or intent to bring about the results you desire.

- **Karmic actions** won't disappear on their own. You must experience the results, whether good or bad, or purify them through spiritual practices.

Even if you don't believe in karma, treating people with ill intent often leads to hard feelings, which can cause unhappiness and resentment. These feelings alone can cause troubles in life. People often attribute karma to treating others the way you want to be treated.

How to earn good Karma for you? Remember these lessons:

- The hardest thing you will ever do is forgive someone who never apologized. But you don't do this for them, you do it for you.
- You can forgive some people without welcoming them back into your life. Apology accepted. Access denied.
- Think of life as a game. We can't undo a move, but we can make the next one better.
- Remain indifferent towards people and situations, let it not affect you in any way.
- You don't need to change the world around you. You need to change how you see.
- Teach your heart to accept disappointments. Even from people you love.
- You can't heal in the same environment that made you sick.
- Stop trying to make the wrong people love you the right way.
- Surround yourself with people who are going to lift you higher.
- The best revenge is no revenge. Move on. Be happy.

When Alexander the Great was dying, He called his Generals and told them his three final wishes.

The first wish: Only the very best doctors should carry my coffin.
The second wish: Scatter my wealth on the road to the graveyard.
The third wish was: Leave my hand hanging in the wind for everyone to see.

His Generals were shocked and asked him to explain. Alexander replied: I want doctors to carry my coffin to show that even the best doctors are powerless to cure in front of death. I want the road scattered with my wealth so everybody can see that riches gained on earth, will stay on earth. I want my hand to wing freely in the wind so that people understand that we are born empty-handed & we leave empty handed after what's most precious is gone: Time.

As per my Guru, Karma can be performed by engaging various faculties. Based on faculty used to perform the karma they are divided into in three different categories namely -

1. Mental Actions

These are the actions performed mentally or simply put thoughts (मानसकि कर्म), but are not accompanied by physical action. Examples are sitting idly and thinking, or actions performed in our dreams when the senses are not cognizant. Without the senses the mind performs numerous possible and even impossible actions.

2. Mental plus Physical Actions

These are those karma when one is mentally engaged, and physical actions accompany it. These are performed in wakeful consciousness state for example, reading an article falls in this category.

3. Physical Actions

Physical actions are those where one puts on an act while hiding one's inner feelings. For example, you might abhor some person; yet motivated by some personal gain, you pretend to be happy to see him. You extend a warm welcome even though you were upset and unwilling to welcome him. In this case, welcoming the person is a mere physical action and the actual feeling for the person is the work of the mind.

God only takes note of the thoughts in your mind and disregards your physical activity. Mind alone is the cause of suffering or liberation. We do not get any result of actions performed in our dreams or our physical actions.

When a bird is alive, it eats ants. When the bird is dead, ants eat the bird. Time and circumstances can change at any time. Don't devalue or hurt anyone in your life. You may be powerful today, but remember time is more powerful than you. One tree makes a million match sticks. Only one matchstick is needed to burn a million trees. So be good and do good because when Karma lands, it lands hard.

We are not taking any material possessions that we have acquired in this life. We are only taking the Karma. Choice is ours. Whether we want to earn good karma or bad karma.

My Guru emphasized that we should reprimand ourselves immediately as any feeling of anger, jealousy, lust, or greed overpowers us. We should remind ourselves that our Guru and God are watching us, and if we have all these vices, how can we receive their grace?

"The meaning of Karma is in the intention. The intention behind action is what matters." – Bhagvad Gita

Sources

- Bhagvad Gita

- Bhagavata

- Discourses of Shree Kripalu Ji Maharaj

- American Buddhist - Thubten Chodron

- Childhood Stories

- Inspiration from friends

- Influences from Work

- Influences from Personal life.